THE TREE OUTSIDE THE WINDOW

The Tree
Outside the Window:
Doris Lessing's
Children of Violence

by
Ellen Cronan Rose

Published for Dartmouth College
by the University Press of New England
Hanover, New Hampshire, 1976

Produced and distributed *on demand* by University
Microfilms International, Ann Arbor, Michigan 48106.
The editorial content of this book has been evaluated,
and the book approved for publication by the editorial
and governing boards of the University Press of New
England.

Library of Congress Cataloging in Publication Data

Rose, Ellen Cronan, 1938-
 The tree outside the window.

 (Monograph publishing on demand : Imprint series)
 Bibliography: p.
 Includes index.
 1. Lessing, Doris May, 1919-   Children of violence.
2. Psychological fiction. I. Title.

PR6023.E833C537   823'.9'14   76-44671
ISBN 0-8357-0189-1

ACKNOWLEDGMENTS

I would like to thank Professors Lee R. Edwards, Cynthia Griffin Wolff, and Eric M. Beekman of the University of Massachusetts for their generous support and invaluable criticism during the epigenesis of this study. A modified version of Chapter 7 appeared in *Hartford Studies in Literature*, and I am grateful to its editor, Leonard Manheim, for helping me to a clearer formulation of my ideas than I had initially articulated.

To the Faculty Research Committee of Dartmouth College, I am indebted for a grant that helped make publication of this study possible. And to my children, Emily, Amanda, and Barnabas, I owe a debt I can never repay, the conviction that I could do it at all.

Hanover, N.H.   E.C.R.
May 1976

CONTENTS

THE TREE OUTSIDE THE WINDOW

1. ERIKSON AND THE *BILDUNGSROMAN*

In the Author's Notes which conclude *The Four-Gated City*, Doris Lessing writes, "this book is what the Germans call a *Bildungsroman*."[1] The Germans, who invented and perfected the form, call Goethe's *Wilhelm Meister* the first *bildungsroman*. Wilhelm's aim is "the cultivation of my individual self, here as I am."[2] The *Lehrjahre* documents his discovery and affirmation of his essential identity through a series of testing encounters with the world. These adventures and their sequence have established a generic pattern that structures at least the first four books of *Children of Violence*, where a proud rebellious adolescent from the provinces, linked in some mystical way with her native soil but electing to seek her fortune in the perilous city, encounters a series of adventures (job, sex, marriage, motherhood), accepts the guidance of various mentors (the Cohens, Stella, Anton), is enrolled in a secret society (the Communist Party), and finally, like Stephen Dedalus, escapes the confining nets of provincial Africa and takes wing across the seas to London and the unspecified self-fulfillment it embodies. But in what possible way can Lessing's account in *The Four-Gated City* of Martha's middle age be aligned with this familiar pattern of the adolescent coming of age? At least one critic has pointed out that *The Four-Gated City* begins *after* most *bildungsromane* end.[3]

In discussing the *bildungsroman*, it is easy to confuse vehicle with tenor, form with content. The pattern of the hero's adventures is less important than the process it embodies, a process Martha describes in *The Four-Gated City* as "a curve of growth . . . there is a central pressure, like sap forcing up a trunk, along a branch, into last year's wood, and there, from a dead-looking eye or knot, it bursts again in a new branch, in a shape that is inevitable but known only to itself until it becomes visible" (p. 192). As a novel of development or growth, *The Four-Gated City* is as much a *bildungsroman* as the four volumes that precede it.

Martha's idea of growth is a lay statement of the embryological principle of epigenesis, which replaces the medieval notion of the homunculus with a concept of fetal development, by which each organ has its time of origin in a predetermined sequence. Erik Erikson has extended the principle of epigenesis from embryology to psychology as the process by which the normal child grows to maturity according to "inner laws of development." These laws dictate that each stage of development is related to all others, and "that they all depend on the proper development in the proper sequence of each item."[4]

Merely to list his "Eight Ages of Man" does an injustice to Erikson but may serve at least to indicate the sequential development in time of the mature and integrated personality.

The accomplishment of early infancy is a sense of basic trust, rooted in the mutuality of recognition between the hungry infant and his nurturing mother. Early childhood brings a sense of autonomy, as the child assumes control of his bodily functions and thus is able to test his will against the demands of others. The active toddler acquires a sense of initiative as he tests various roles in his fantasy and play. When he enters school, the child acquires a sense of industry as he becomes intrigued with making things work. The accomplishment of adolescence is the formation of a sense of identity which subsumes the childhood identity elements of trust, autonomy, initiative, and industry, and forms the necessary basis for the accomplishments of maturity.

"Beyond identity" in the life cycle are the tasks and accruing strengths of adulthood. The first is intimacy, in which the young adult who is sure of his identity develops a close, reciprocal relationship with another. Next is generativity, the assumption of responsibility for the next generation, whether in actual parenthood or in general altruism and creativity. And the final and by no means inevitable achievement of the vital personality is a sense of integrity, the wisdom of old age.

Most *bildungsromane* end with Erikson's fifth age, with the hero poised on the brink of adulthood, confidently stretching his wings. But the adult Martha's personal relationships in *The Four-Gated City* both reveal and extend the idiosyncratic curve of her growth. If the epigenetic principle asserts the sequential development of a sense of identity, it also inevitably implies that imperfect achievement at any early stage will distort subsequent growth. *The Four-Gated City* reveals Martha's fundamental failure to achieve a sense of basic trust. This handicap has dictated the style of her growth through work, sexual adventure, and political affiliation. Now it distorts her adult relationships as well, as she sustains her identity crisis beyond adolescence into efforts at intimacy and exercises of generative responsibility.

Erikson's epigenetic theory of development is a significant modification of Freud's description of psychosexual development. Nothing he says about basic trust counters what Freud says about orality, but the needs, fulfillments, and frustrations of this period are more complex and problematic than we had thought. Not only is the infant compelled by his own organic desires and capacities, but he is reacted to and interpreted by a particular mother and a general consensus about acceptable feeding patterns. How secure that consensus is, how far the mother accepts it, and how adequate it may be to a particular infant's needs—these three factors combine with the sheer erotic pleasure of sucking to form a developmental stage we call oral.

Freud's is a closed system; instinctual energy is transferred from one object to another according to Newtonian laws of conservation. Erikson augments Freud by recognizing the equally potent influence on individual development of the interaction between self and society. The mature adult is the sum of more than his libidinal energies, expressed, repressed, or sublimated. He has also passed through significant encounters with society, in which his developing capacities, intellectual as well as organic, are tested and either supported or thwarted by those around him. Under optimum conditions these encounters comprise a sequence of growth, by which each stage consolidates former achievements and in turn lays the foundation for further development.

This dialectic between self and society is central to the *bildungsroman*. Although Wilhelm Meister's aim is "the cultivation of my individual self, here as I am," he does not develop *in vacuo*. His adventures are essential to his self-development because there is a reciprocity between external events and his inner nature. The *bildungsroman* refutes the old idea of the homunculus with a dynamic of growth, a dialectic between what Hans Castorp calls the "little something" within and the "outward pressure" of events.[5]

As Erikson demonstrates, the little something within each of us which makes us unique is continually vulnerable to the pressure of outward events. Clinically speaking, herein lies man's hope, and his doom. The sins of the father may be redeemed by our neighbor. Given new social contexts, larger than the original family nucleus, we may free ourselves of the curse of our infantile traumas, as we work out new and creative ways of interacting with an ever-expanding environment. Less optimistically, if society does not provide an arena for growth, the individual is condemned to repeat whatever patterns of need and frustration his infancy established.

Martha Quest's initial encounter with the world in the person of her mother failed to establish in her that sense of trust which is fundamental to a sense of identity. Instead, it endowed her with a mode of relating to other people which continues to characterize her as she matures. And the world she perceives offers her repeated opportunities to exercise her dominant modality of interaction, to remain a psychological infant.

However densely populated and convincingly realistic the world of *Children of Violence* may be, Martha remains the center of interest. It is not motherhood that is at issue in *A Proper Marriage,* but Martha's temptation to abandon the arduous search for herself and assume the collective and protective identity of a "warm, large, delightful, maternal, humorous female . . . like a queen ant."[6] *A Ripple from the Storm* is a statement not about

Communism, but about that stage in Martha's development in which "she lived in 'the group' and did not care about the judgements of anyone else."[7] It may be true that society offers only limited opportunities to women, but what Lessing shows us is Martha's interpretation of these limitations and her reaction to them. The world we live in may well be fragmented and chaotic, but the interest in *The Four-Gated City* centers on Martha's perception of this world and her way of coming to terms with it.

However accurate it may or may not be, Martha's perception of society is that it is hostile. The world of the early volumes of *Children of Violence*, with its fixed patterns of domestic and social behavior, is both repugnant and fatally attractive to Martha. Rationally she protests that its rigidity hampers the growth of her "free spirit"; at the same time, because of her unresolved infantile needs, she is drawn to the security it seems to offer her. With that part of herself which is struggling to overcome her psychic handicap, no less than with that part which mistakenly claims to be objective, Martha must hold herself in opposition to her world. At the end of *Landlocked*, she leaves it.

But the world of *The Four-Gated City* is equally uncongenial to her. What threatens her now is not a repressively orderly society, but a world she perceives as fragmented and incoherent. In both political and domestic life, she sees reality belied by appearance. Martha's sense of her own identity is threatened by the world she perceives; she can maintain it only by retreating from the world to the confines of Mark Coldridge's house.

But according to Erikson, one achieves a sense of identity when the "style of one's individuality" is corroborated by "one's meaning for significant others in the immediate community" (*Identity*, p. 50). Ideally the dialectic of growth is resolved in a synthesis of mutual confirmation; as Georg Lukács points out, Wilhelm Meister finds "responses to the innermost demands of his soul in the structures of society."[8] The theme of Goethe's *bildungsroman*, he goes on, is "the reconciliation of the problematic individual, guided by his lived experience of the ideal, with concrete social reality" (p. 132). The underlying assumption which makes the exposition of this theme possible is that there is a correspondence between reality and social organization; the questing hero, when he reaches the end of the educative process, discovers that his identity and its social articulation are synonymous.

At the end of the novel Wilhelm Meister assumes paternity and the responsibility for educating his son, thus taking his place in the sequence of generations and demonstrating the twofold relation of self to society inherent in Erikson's definition of identity. The individual achieves a sense of identity when his self-image is confirmed by his society. He maintains his sense of identity by making it operative, by turning from the mirror and facing the future. For Erikson identity is an adolescent achievement. The mature person must go beyond it to assume responsibility in the cycle of generations because "only an adult ethics can guarantee to the next generation an equal chance to experience the full cycle of humanness" (*Identity*, p. 42).

Goethe's *bildungsroman* postulates "the possibility of human and interior community among men, of understanding and common action in respect of the essential" (Lukács, p. 133). This means not only that one's behavior in society will be correctly perceived as an expression of oneself, but that activity in society will be fully engaging and enhancing of the self one uniquely is. At least in Carlyle's translation, *Wilhelm Meister* continually asserts a preference for the active over the contemplative life, condemning all retirement from the world. The saintly Canonness, the Count who joins the Hernhuth community, the Harper whose bizarre dress distinguishes him from ordinary men, and above all Wilhelm's playacting[9] are all strictured by the activists of the Society of the Tower who define the moral dimensions of the novel. *Wilhelm Meister* does not echo Christ's assertion that in order to find himself, a man must lose himself. But it does contend that, having discovered his identity, a man must transcend himself in service to others. In the words of one of the leaders of the Society of the Tower:

> It is right that a man, when he first enters upon life, should think highly of himself, should determine to attain many eminent distinctions, should endeavor to make all things possible: but when his education has proceeded to a certain pitch, it is advantageous for him that he learn to lose himself among a mass of men, that he learn to live for the sake of others, and to forget himself in an activity prescribed by duty. (p. 444)

Wilhelm Meister is the first *bildungsroman*. In its harmonious reconciliation between the self and the world, it is also unique. Since the Enlightenment, the world has become uncongenial, and virtually all *bildungsromane* written after Goethe's document the pessimistic education of the hero to the impossibility of realizing his identity within the forms of a moribund or hostile society. Denied the happy synthesis that marks the end of Wilhelm's quest, these heroes are "lonely" because they discover that "the desire for the essence always leads out of the world of social structures and communities and that a community is possible only at the surface of life and can only be based on compromise" (Lukács, p. 136). Those who refuse to compromise, like Maggie Tulliver and Jude Fawley, die. Society will not tolerate the identity they achieve, and if their deaths are not a moral victory, they are certainly a practical victory for society. As the avatar exits, the irritant is removed, and things go on more or less as they were.

But the mood of most post-Goethian *bildungsromane* is not so much tragic as resigned, as the hero "accommodates himself to society by resigning himself to accept its life forms, and by locking inside himself and keeping entirely to himself the interiority which can only be realized inside the soul" (Lukács, p. 136).

A more optimistic solution to the conflict between the individual and society is outlined by Erikson himself in his two nonfiction *bildungsromane, Young Man Luther* and *Gandhi's Truth.* Luther's and Gandhi's achievement of a full and functioning sense of identity was possible because, however inarticulately, they perceived a similarity between their own pathologies and their ailing societies. By seizing the inchoate world around them and remolding it into a congenial shape, by creating their own facilitating environment for growth, they became leaders. And thus, as Erikson says of Luther, they lifted their "individual patienthood to the level of a universal one" and [solved] for all what [they] could not solve for [themselves] alone."[10] In a sense this is what Stephen Dedalus sets out to do at the end of his *bildung,* as he vows "to forge in the smithy of my soul the uncreated conscience of my race."

What all *bildungsromane* have in common is their acceptance of the equivalent reality of self and society. The hero can end his quest for identity by returning to the fold or by striking off on his own. But in some way he must come to terms with a world which implacably exists, and which either affirms or rejects him. He may, as Wilhelm and his friend Lothario pledge themselves to do, reform abuses. He may even turn his back on the world. But he cannot make it go away.

At the end of *Landlocked,* Martha has not achieved a sense of identity. Crippled by the unsatisfactoriness of her original encounter with the world around her, Martha perceives that world as hostile. As it does not seem to her to have facilitated her growth to self-understanding, so it has for her no confirming power. Martha regards the "forms of ordinary life merely as tools" (FG, p. 428) for carving her identity. Thus she makes the world around her less real than her self. And thus, paradoxically, she prevents herself from achieving a sense of identity which, as Erikson has shown, must be a reflective as well as a reflexive accomplishment.

In *The Four-Gated City* Lessing depicts Martha's sustained identity crisis. What we are shown is a hero who would be a Luther or a Gandhi, who would resolve the conflict between her self and her uncongenial environment by refashioning the world. But as Lessing clearly demonstrates, Martha's reformulations of reality all manifest her dominant modality of interaction. They recapitulate, even as they try to refashion, her unresolved infantile needs.

Furthermore, Martha is portrayed by Lessing in *The Four-Gated City* as capable of relating only to a context she herself defines. In Mark Coldridge's house Martha finds a community that seems to authenticate her and thus to verify her sense of identity. In that house, as well, she turns her sense of her self to the service of others. But Mark's house is not the world and, in the end, it is demolished by an order from the London County Council. Having refused to acknowledge and come to terms with the world around her, Martha is left an isolate at the novel's end, doomed to continue her quest for identity.

But the novel has a second ending, and there Lessing's clearsighted vision of Martha and her precise understanding of the components of identity go askew. The apocalyptic appendix of the novel, in which Martha founds a new society upon the wreckage of the old, suggests that Lessing has been seduced by her protagonist, that she shares Martha's belief that what really exists is less real than what one wills to exist. One reason why *The Four-Gated City* is a failed *bildungsroman* may be that its creator has misapprehended her powers. Instead of refashioning the world like Gandhi or Luther, she has replaced it with a Utopia of her own devising. At least we are prevented by history from assessing the durability of the bridge she constructs over the chasm that looms between her protagonist and present reality. Looking backward, we can see that Luther and Gandhi devised original and politically viable patterns of relationship between the individual and society; looking forward, we are as free to speculate as Lessing, and no more able than she to prophesy.

The question of how far Lessing shares Martha's attitude toward the world cannot be answered with reference only to *The Four-Gated City,* or even to *Children of Violence* as a whole. Lessing's preoccupation with artistic creation—and re-creation—is central to *The Golden Notebook* and implicit in nearly everything she has written. How far she shares her protagonists' perception of the world as "fragmented," to what extent she believes it can and should be healed, and by what means, aesthetic or political—these are questions beyond the scope of this investigation.

What I will, instead, be concerned to delineate is Lessing's central concern in *Children of Violence* with Martha Quest's growth toward a sense of identity. Insofar as this is also the central concern of the *bildungsroman,* to which genre Lessing has committed at least the final volume of the series, it is appropriate to attempt to align *Children of Violence* with the genre. Whether Martha Quest achieves Wilhelm Meister's successful synthesis of the dialectic of growth in and through society, whether she is then able to act in and for society—these are questions Lessing raises and with which I will be concerned.

In my reading of *Children of Violence* I have found Eriksonian ego-psychology, with its bifocal attention to individual development and the interaction between the individual and society, continually illuminating. If my study of the Martha Quest series should suggest the applicability of Erikson's theories to the *bildungsroman* in particular and to literary criticism in general, it will have justified itself.

As a critic, I have been both admonished and consoled by Erikson's reminder that "wherever you begin, you will have to begin again twice over."[11] I have by no means said the final word about *Children of Violence*.

2. THE EPIGENESIS OF MARTHA'S IDENTITY

In *The Four-Gated City,* Martha asks her psychiatrist, Dr. Lamb, for
a diagnosis. His answer is unhesitating: "You're manic-depressive, with schizoid tendencies" (p. 226). He reassures her that this "doesn't mean that you
are two people," and indeed the schizoid split is more radical than any Jekyll
and Hyde configuration. For R. D. Laing, "the term schizoid refers to an individual the totality of whose experience is split in two main ways: in the
first place, there is a rent in his relation with his world and, in the second,
there is a disruption of his relation with himself."[1] The schizoid lacks "primary ontological security" (p. 39), the experience of "his own being as real,
alive, whole; as differentiated from the rest of the world in ordinary circumstances so clearly that his identity and autonomy are never in question; as a
continuum in time; as having an inner consistency, substantiality, genuine-
ness, and worth; as spatially co-extensive with the body" (p. 41). The schizoid is troubled not with multiple identities but with the lack of any identity.

Laing translates into phenomenological language what Erikson prefers
to discuss in basic English. For both a sense of identity is "conjunctive" (*The
Divided Self,* p. 41). "The conscious feeling of having a personal identity is
based on two simultaneous observations: the perception of the selfsameness
and continuity of one's existence in time and space and the perception of
the fact that others recognize one's sameness and continuity" (*Identity,*
p. 50). Thus the cohesion of one's personal sense of identity depends on a
sustaining mutuality with others or, in the language of phenomenology, "if a
man is not two-dimensional, having a two-dimensional identity established
by a conjunction of identity-for-others, and identity-for-oneself, if he does
not exist objectively as well as subjectively, but has only a subjective identity, an identity-for-himself, he cannot be *real*" (*The Divided Self,* p. 95).[2]

For both Laing and Erikson the foundations of this sense of personal
identity are laid in early infancy, when the baby is "existentially born as real
and alive" (*The Divided Self,* p. 41). This second birth, as fraught as the first
with traumatic possibilities, is into a world of relationships, as the newborn's
"inborn and more or less coordinated ability to take in by mouth meets the
mother's more or less co-ordinated ability and intention to feed him and to
welcome him" (*Identity,* p. 97). Under optimum circumstances the infant
will carry with him from this initial encounter with the world a sense of

basic trust, a reliance on the authenticity of his own needs and on the ability and willingness of others to answer them. But if the baby's trust is violated, if he is exposed to excessive frustration or unassimilable largesse, if he is not verified in his needs by his mother's response, he is left with an abiding sense of basic mistrust, a disruption of his relation with himself as a trustworthy person because of a rent in his relation with the world in the person of his mother. For Erikson no less than for Laing, "a radical impairment of basic trust and a prevalence of basic mistrust is expressed in a particular form of severe estrangement" (*Identity*, p. 97) which we call schizoid.[3]

Characterizing stages of development by modes of behavior rather than zones of erogenous gratification, Erikson distinguishes two successive components of Freud's oral phase. The first, in which the baby gets what is given and thus establishes through a mutual relationship a sense of basic trust and a rudimentary sense of his identity, is succeeded by a second incorporative phase whose identifying mode is taking and holding. The infant can bite with his new teeth, can grasp with his newly focused vision, can thus add to his nascent sense of identity the rudiments of autonomous will. In most cultures this phase coincides with weaning, which, "even under the most favorable circumstances . . . seems to introduce into psychic life (and become prototypical for) a sense of inner division and universal nostalgia for a paradise forfeited" (*Childhood and Society*, p. 250). When the infant's prior experience of mutuality with a nurturing other has been blighted, this anxiety is exacerbated and becomes symptomatic.

Children of Violence is not a case history, and Martha is Dr. Lamb's patient, not ours. But even to the amateur Freudian, *Children of Violence* offers abundant evidence of Martha's orality. On the most primitive level it is apparent in her problematic attitude toward food. Food is never simply fuel for Martha. It is a threat to her stylish and unnatural slimness on the one hand (e.g., MQ, pp. 83, 110, 116; PM, p. 158),[4] while on the other it provides inordinate comfort. Her favorite foods are nursery treats, "slabs of chocolate" (MQ, p. 110), which she devours, like a child, until they make her sick. She and Adolph King, her first lover, spend New Year's Day "lying on the bed and eating chocolates" (MQ, p. 185). Even as a sexually sophisticated thirty-year-old, Martha prefaces her love-making with Jack with a mug of hot cocoa (FG, pp. 47–48).

When her escort to a Sports Club party neglects to give her dinner before the dance, she interprets this not as a stinginess but as rejection: "so it was that, at the very beginning of the evening, she was separated from Donovan; it was rather as if he had pushed her away" (MQ, p. 151). On the other hand, she supposes that Anton loves her because he fusses over her meals, ordering for her, scolding her for not taking care of herself (RS, pp. 49, 172).

She declares her allegiances through the meals she shares and rejects people by refusing to eat with them.[5] Her struggles with her infant daughter over food document her rejection of the maternal role.[6]

Martha reads as she eats chocolates, "like a famished person, cramming into the shortest possible time a truly remarkable quantity of vicarious experience" (MQ, p. 200). Her first months of political activity are similarly "crammed" (RS, p. 18) with new sensations, and when the group dissolves at the end of *A Ripple from the Storm*, "Martha felt herself cut off from everything that had fed her imagination" (p. 259).

But even more than by a ravening hunger, Martha is characterized by her sense of inner division, "as if half a dozen entirely different people inhabited her body" (MQ, p. 143), which she assuages by "indulging in the forbidden pleasure of nostalgia" (PM, p. 129). What she yearns for is an identity that will unify the fragments of her self.

The foundations of identity are laid in infancy, with the basic trust that is the infant's first exercise in mutuality. The nursing infant learns to discriminate between himself and the "enduring quality of the thing world." He experiences "the caretaking person as a coherent being,"[7] who responds to his needs and thus authenticates them and him. If the psychosocial gains of early infancy are imperfectly consolidated, the individual's "nostalgia" for the paradise we all forfeit at our weaning becomes a longing for something he has never had. Martha's nostalgia is for the symbiosis that precedes identity formation, a "strong impulse of longing" Freud calls oceanic, "anonymous, impersonal, formless, like water" (MQ, p. 143).

Lacking a sense of herself as discrete and delimited, Martha makes one attempt after another to merge into some greater identity. She is as formless and undefined as her body, which is "thin as a bone one month and as fat as a pig the next" (PM, p. 2). Passively she drifts into marriage, "gone on the tide . . . half drowned in champagne . . . completely swept away by it all" (MQ, pp. 226–227). She "lapse[s] into" motherhood "as into a sea" (PM, p. 275), thus gaining entry into a "community of women, all so much older than herself, all absorbed into the rhythm of eating, sleeping, and nursing" (PM, p. 150). Unsatisfied by marriage and motherhood, she turns to Communism for a sense of "exaltation" (RS, p. 30), and when she fails to find it there, she turns to sex. Feeling "self-divided" (RS, p. 39), she longs for a man who will "[create] her, [allow] her to be her 'self'—but a new self, since it is his conception which forms her" (RS, p. 38). Into this vacuum walks Thomas Stern, with whom she is "dissolved" (LL, p. 99) by a fusion so complete that they "[put] into words each other's thoughts" (LL, p. 219).

Unlike other *bildungsromane—David Copperfield, Great Expectations, The Mill on the Floss, A Portrait of the Artist as a Young Man*, to cite only the most obvious—*Children of Violence* does not evoke the protagonist's childhood. Perhaps Martha's memories are too painful to recall; her parents have never witheld from her the "information that she was unwanted in the first place" (MQ, p. 239). "Yet that uncomfortably antagonistic childhood had over it a shimmering haze of beauty, it tugged at her to return" (PM, p. 129). What tugs at her is the memory of "that experience (she thought of it as one, though it was the fusion of many, varying in intensity) which was the gift of her solitary childhood on the veld" (MQ, p. 200), an experience she has internalized as "her lodestone, even her conscience" (MQ, p. 200).

Her groping attempt to describe that experience is worth quoting at length, because it both illustrates her regressive longing for fusion with a greater, more meaningful identity than her own fragmented experience of her self and suggests the dimensions of the problem she confronts as a developing ego, deprived of its infantile foundation of basic trust:

> What she had been waiting for like a revelation was a pain, not a happiness; what she remembered, always, was the exultation and the achievement, what she forgot was this difficult birth into a state of mind which words like *ecstasy, illumination,* and so on could not describe, because they suggest joy . . . such experiences were common among the religious . . .
>
> There was certainly a definite point at which the thing began. It was not; then it was suddenly inescapable, and nothing could have frightened it away. There was a slow integration, during which she, and the little animals, and the moving grasses, and the sunwarmed trees, and the slopes of shivering silvery mealies, and the great dome of blue light overhead, and the stones of earth under her feet, became one, shuddering together in a dissolution of dancing atoms. She felt the rivers under the ground forcing themselves painfully along her veins, swelling them out in an unbearable pressure; her flesh was the earth, and suffered growth like a ferment; and her eyes stared, fixed like the eye of the sun. Not for one second longer (if the terms for time apply) could she have borne it; but then, with a sudden movement forwards and out, the whole process stopped; and *that* was the "moment" which it was impossible to remember afterwards. For during that space of time (which was timeless) she understood quite finally her smallness, the unimportance of humanity. In her ears was an inchoate grinding, the great wheels of movement, and it was inhuman, like the blundering rocking movement of a bullock cart; and no part of that sound was Martha's voice . . . For that moment, while space and time (but these are words, and if she understood anything it was that words, here, were like the sound of a baby crying in a whirlwind) kneaded her flesh, she knew futility; that is, what was futile was her own idea of herself and her place in the chaos of matter. What was demanded of her was that she should accept something quite different; it was as if something new was demanding conception, with her flesh as host; as if it were a necessity, which she must bring herself to accept, that she should allow herself to dissolve and be formed by that necessity. (MQ, pp. 52–53)

Clearly Martha thinks of this childhood "revelation," the "measure" (MQ, p. 200) by which she evaluates her adult experience, as a mystical loss of self. If she can merge her insignificant self into a greater whole, the "futility" of trying to establish a sense of identity becomes an occasion for joy, rather than despair. Not only is this ontologically reassuring, but (like certain mystical experiences) sensually gratifying as well. The cadences of Martha's prose evoke the sex act, as do the words she uses to describe the experience: "There was certainly a definite point at which the thing began. It was not; then it was suddenly inescapable, and nothing could have frightened it away. There was a slow integration, during which she, and the little animals, and the moving grasses, and the sunwarmed trees, and the slopes of shivering silvery mealies, and the great dome of blue light overhead, and the stones of earth under her feet"—each phrase accumulating more adjectives, the thrusting rhythm becoming slower and more insistent until the abrupt predicate— "became one"—and the post-coital "shudder" of relaxation. The act occurs twice in succession, as Martha tries again to describe the sensation of the experience, this time emphasizing the almost unbearably painful tension of the coital act, with its culminating orgasmic relief as "with a sudden movement forwards and out, the whole process stopped; and *that* was the 'moment' which it was impossible to remember afterwards." Like the Virgin, Martha has been miraculously impregnated; her glory is her passive surrender to a necessity and an identity greater than herself.

But the words and rhythms of sex can be read another way, retrospectively, from the metaphor of conception. From this perspective, the passage describes a birth. The rhythmic contractions of the prose are labor pangs, and the sudden movement forward and out are the expulsion of the newborn child.

This is an instance of meaningful ambiguity. Martha's "illumination" is both a synopsis of her handicap and a statement of her task. As the questing here of a *bildungsroman*, Martha must find and assert her identity. But a sense of identity rests on the fundamental distinction between oneself and others: one must, as one grows, become increasingly more separate. The infant's sense of basic trust in a nurturing other is the cornerstone and model for his subsequent individuation. Lacking this rudimentary sense of identity, Martha must be reborn. Fighting against the seductive nostalgia for symbiotic fusion, Martha must give birth to herself.

I will return to this positive aspect of Martha's illumination in a later chapter. For now it may be enough to indicate that this necessity to give birth to her own identity is the source both of the plot and of the essential optimism of *Children of Violence*. For just as Erikson's psychology stresses the creative and adaptive resilience of the ego, so does Lessing document not Martha's victimization, but her growth.

In an interview with Roy Newquist in 1964, Lessing described her one mescaline "trip" as an experience of giving birth, in which she was both the mother and the baby. "Looking back," she says, "I think that my very healthy psyche decided that my own birth, the one I actually had, was painful and bad . . . and the birth 'I' invented for myself was not painful."[8]

The problem of the numerous "I's" involved in the birth—the mother, the baby, the attendants—is what Lessing calls a writer's problem, and she goes on to discuss the difficulty she had in creating the various selves of Anna Wulf in *The Golden Notebook*. "But that creature being born wasn't a 'writer.' It was immensely ancient, for a start, and it was neither male nor female, and it had no race nor nationality. I can revive the 'feel' or 'taste' of that creature fairly easily. It isn't far off that creature or person you are when you wake up from deep sleep, and for a moment you don't recognize your surroundings and you think: Who am I? Where am I? Is this my hand? You're somebody, all right, but who?" (*Counterpoint*, p. 424).

You're somebody, all right, but who? Answering that question is Martha's five-volume task. "Identity formation," says Erikson, "is a process of increasing differentiation . . . which 'begins' somewhere in the first true 'meeting' of mother and baby as two persons who can touch and recognize each other, and . . . does not 'end' until a man's power of mutual affirmation wanes" (*Identity*, pp. 22–23).

As we have seen Martha's identity formation never truly began. Although Lessing does not evoke her childhood, we can infer Martha's imperfect resolution of the initial infantile crisis—resulting in that sense of basic trust which is the foundation of identity—from her adult orality and nostalgia. Before I try to show Martha's remarkable feat in answering the question "You're somebody, all right, but who?" let me examine the crippling handicap she has to surmount.

In discussing neurotic behavior, Freud emphasized the individual's libidinal fixation on erogenous zones (mouth, anus, genitals), but Erikson focuses on modal fixation. In other words, the adult compulsive is not acting out a sphincter or zonal fixation so much as he is replicating in his daily life a mode of behavior which first became crucial in the anal phase of his early childhood, a response to people, things, and experience in which he alternatively holds on and lets go. Thus it is that Martha, who has been originally and damagingly deprived of a sense of basic trust, retains incorporation as her characteristic mode. What Lessing describes, and what Erikson invites us to think through, is an arc of development shaped by Martha's need "*to get, not in the sense of 'go and get' but in that of receiving and accepting what is given*" (*Identity*, p. 99).

As a mode of interacting with the environment, what Freud designates as the anal phase "becomes a battle for autonomy" (*Identity*, p. 108), in which the infant's will is tested against the expectations and desires of the parents who train him. "For the growth of autonomy," says Erikson, "a firmly developed early trust is necessary. The infant must have come to be sure that his faith in himself and in the world will not be jeopardized by the violent wish to have his choice, to appropriate demandingly, and to eliminate stubbornly" (*Identity*, p. 110). Even more important to the development of autonomy than trust in others is the infant's sense of his own trustworthiness. In order to exercise his will, he relies on that aspect of basic trust which assures him that he is a separate being, with urges of his own and the capacity, however unsophisticated, to deal with them.

Martha, as we have seen, has no sense of her self. She feels both "fragmented" and "formless." She achieves an imperfect sense of autonomy because, failing to define the boundaries of her self, she is unable to will anything for herself. Without a fundamental sense of the distinction between herself and others, she confuses the will of others for her own. She is not what she wills but what others will her to be.

For phenomenologists this aspect of autonomy is related to "bodiliness." We assert our uniqueness when we learn not that we *have* bodies, but that we *are* our bodies. This is what Gabriel Marcel calls the "existential indubitable."[9] Laing characterizes the schizoid personality as "the divided self," the unincarnate being, whose "self" is "unembodied" (*The Divided Self*, chapter 4) and in extreme cases in violent opposition to his body.

In one sense Martha does not even "have" a body. In order to see herself, "she would take [her] mirror to her parents' bedroom, and hold it at an angle to the one at the window, and examine herself, at this double remove." Even then, "she could see herself only in sections" (MQ, p. 16). Not knowing what she looks like, Martha lets herself be dressed and formed by others, first by her mother, who distorts and disguises Martha's maturing body in "childish dresses" (MQ, p. 16), later by Donovan, who treats her like a mannequin and for whom she adorns her body "under the power of that compulsion that seemed to come from outside, as if Donovan's dark and languid eyes were dictating what she must do" (MQ, p. 98).

By the time of her marriage to Douglas, Martha has learned that she has a body, but it is an unruly possession. "It was almost with the feeling of a rider who was wondering whether his horse would make the course that she regarded this body of hers, which was not only divided from her brain by the necessity of keeping open that cool and dispassionate eye, but separated into compartments of its own" (PM, p. 63). Tutored by a marriage manual, Martha learns to manipulate her body, but "her mind was anxiously aware, not only of a disconnected partner, a body, but of every part of it, which might or might not come up to scratch at any given occasion" (PM, p. 63).

Instead of developing an autonomous will to assert and project her self to others, Martha incorporates the world's standards as will-power;[10] her self, defined by others, denies the authenticity of her own body.

But although Martha passively allows herself to be molded and directed by parents, boy friends, and books, she is occasionally rebellious. Feeling confined and frustrated by her schoolgirl clothes, she cuts them short (MQ,

p. 16). When she is older, she sews a dance dress that provocatively reveals "her naked brown shoulders slightly tensed" (MQ, p. 69) in a gesture of defiance against her mother's notion of what nice girls wear. Though she submits to Donovan's expert direction, she "shudder[s] with dislike of him" (MQ, p. 145), and she wonders whether the marriage manual view of her body as a machine isn't "an offense against what was deepest and most real in her" (PM, p. 63).

But since she has no grounds for knowing what is deepest and most real in herself, since she has not even a rudimentary sense of her embodied self, her moments of rebellion are short lived. More characteristically, she feels the shame and self-doubt that Erikson describes as the "dynamic counterpart" (*Childhood and Society*, p. 274) of the positive psychosocial achievements of the anal stage. Each flash of rebellion is succeeded by a "double take" (*Identity*, p. 112) in which Martha judges her tentative assertion of will by the harsh and unfriendly standards of others. When her gesture of autonomy involves her body, her reaction is one of shame. Cutting off her dresses alarms Mrs. Quest, who attempts to make Martha ashamed of her precociously well-developed figure. That she succeeds, at least in part, is reflected by Martha's dream the night before she is to wear the dance dress she has sewn to defy her mother, a classic dream of shame:[11]

> She was wearing her white frock in a vast ballroom hung with glittering chandeliers, the walls draped with thick rich crimson; and as she walked towards a group of people who stood rather above the floor, in long fluted gowns, like living statues, she noticed a patch of mud on her skirt and, looking down, saw that all her dress was covered with filth. She turned helplessly for flight, when Marnie and her brother came towards her, bent with laughter, their hands pressed over their mouths, gesturing to her that she must escape before the others, those beautiful and legendary beings at the end of the long hall, should catch sight of her. (MQ, p. 68)

The protagonist of a *bildungsroman* is traditionally passive; as Roy Pascal describes him, "the hero is not a man of action or will, he does not influence the march of events." But he does have a "moral personality. In the midst of apparently fortuitous occurrences, he gives the latter a unity within his disposition, he 'moulds' them though he does not cause or control them."[12] Martha, ironically surnamed Quest, has no innate disposition that she can recognize and can see herself only in her parents' mirror. Nothing is more characteristic of her than her lack of initiative. Not only does she shape and dress her body according to other people's definitions of fashion, but she does not even attempt to pass the examination which would take her from the farm she says she hates to the world outside which she dreams of entering (MQ, pp. 20–23). Instead she waits "as if some kind of spell had been put on her" (MQ, p. 23), until Joss Cohen gets her a job in the city with his uncles. Later she thinks of it as "that momentous letter . . . which had released her from her imprisonment like the kiss of the prince in the fairy tales" (MQ, p. 197).

"Doomed, without energy" (MQ, p. 143), Martha is constantly expecting the fairy prince to rescue her. "In a fevered daydream she imagined that some rich and unknown relation would come forward with a hundred pounds, and say, 'Here, Martha Quest, you deserve this, this is to set you free'" (MQ, p. 166). Sometimes the fairy prince is Joss Cohen, at other times his brother Solly "would most certainly help her, rescue her" (PM, p. 37). But most often it is some unspecified man who will "arrive in her life, simply take her by the hand, and lead her off into this new world" (PM, p. 69).

Lacking initiative, Martha fails to develop a sense of industry. At her job she sits idly at her desk, "waiting for someone to direct her" (MQ, p. 95), and although she toys with other, more appealing job possibilities (MQ, pp. 209-212), "a creeping reluctance came over her at the mere idea of two or three years' serious study" (MQ, p. 219).

Initiative and industry are the psychosocial achievements of Freud's Oedipal and latent stages, which Erikson sees as complementary. In the first, the child—whose genitality is "rudimentary" and "not even particularly noticeable"—is characterized by a general intrusiveness. Loud, tireless, perpetually active, he is consumed by curiosity. Within the family constellation, he tries "to comprehend possible future roles." His learning is "vigorous," leading "away from his own limitations and into future possibilities" (Identity, p. 116). The imagination and sense of initiative which are vitalized at this stage of a child's development are channeled into a sense of industry when he reaches school age. Temporarily freed from the overwhelming demands of his libido, he "applies to concrete pursuits and approved goals the drives which have made him dream and play" (Identity, p. 124).

The growing child becomes more aware of an enlarging environment as he becomes less totally the sum of his own libidinal needs. The influences on his development increase in number and become more complex. Thus Martha's lack of initiative and failure to develop a sense of industry are in part a function of her refusal of the roles her society sanctions for women. I will go into this social and sexual aspect of Martha's development in some detail later. But for now, I think it is equally important to distinguish Martha's unique handicap, her infantile and incorporative mode of intercourse with the world expanding around her.

Not only is Martha's progression through the stages of development routed through an infantile mode; it is impeded by a generally regressive tendency. In normal development, the child's imagination is directed away from the unobtainable goals of the Oedipal stage; he learns that "not even in the the distant future is one ever going to be father in sexual relationship to mother, or mother in sexual relationship to father" (*Identity*, p. 117). But Martha replicates the family triangle over and over again in her adult relationships.

Martha's bedroom is adjacent to her parents' and "the door did not lock, or even fasten properly" (MQ, p. 19). The open door characterizes the fluid relationship among these three people. Martha dislikes her mother's cosmetics and "shudder[s] with disgust at [her] touch" (MQ, p. 17), but she aligns herself with her mother against her father, who thinks of them as "a couple of darned fishwives" (MQ, p. 20). At other times Martha sides with her father and "accuse[s] her mother, in her private thoughts, of being responsible" for the diabetes that has made him an invalid (MQ, p. 18). All that is clear in this shifting triangle is that the bonds that form it are strong and deep-seated.

This family configuration is repeated in *The Four-Gated City,* where Martha feels in a sense "married" to Mark, who is Lynda's husband (p. 285). On the other hand, she "hears" Mark's thoughts about Lynda as her own, so that she wonders whether she has a Lesbian attachment for Lynda (pp. 351–352). And at a Ban the Bomb rally, Martha has an uncanny vision of the Mark-Martha-Lynda triangle superimposed on every group of three people who pass by (p. 397). So long as Martha is caught in this family triangle, she is at least partially immobilized. She suffers from a failure of imagination in part because she is looking backward.

But to a greater extent, Martha fails to develop initiative and a sense of industry because intrusiveness is an alien mode. She prefers to let others act for her, to let Joss arrange a job and Stella her love life. But then she suffers from that sense of guilt which is the negative correlative of a sense of initiative. When Mr. Cohen gives her an unearned advance on her salary because "you are an old friend of my nephew," Martha feels "guilty because she had not been a good friend to Joss" (MQ, p. 84). And when she has allowed Stella to get rid of the lover she hasn't courage to dismiss herself, she feels what she calls "shame" but which is much more like guilt: "She said to herself wildly that she must rush down to Adolph's room and say she was sorry, that it had had nothing to do with her, she had not known it was going to be like that" (MQ, p. 195). Martha's guilt reflects her moral inferiority, which itself results from her passivity. And despite its twinge, she feels a "profound thankfulness that [the love affair] was all over. There was no doubt that it was a relief that she need not see him again" (MQ, p. 195).

Martha, who is fifteen when her story begins, remains an adolescent well beyond her majority precisely because "only a firm sense of inner identity marks the end of the adolescent process" (*Identity*, p. 88). Without this sense of identity, there can be no "further and truly individual maturation"

(p. 89), no movement "beyond identity" (p. 135) to the responsibilities of adulthood and the rewards of old age.

Although as Erikson points out and as our survey of Martha's development indicates, identity formation is a process that begins in early infancy, this process "has its normative crisis in adolescence" (p. 23). Contending on the one hand with the revived impulses of his sexuality and on the other with the claims of a society larger and more confusing than the family milieu of his childhood, the adolescent recapitulates his early development. His task is to "integrate" the "identity elements" (p. 128) he has accrued during his childhood into a "new configuration" (p. 159).

But if the individual, like Martha, has not acquired an increment of these identity elements, there is nothing to consolidate. All the basic conflicts—as between trust and mistrust, will and doubt—are revived in virulent form, and "whether or not the ensuing tension will lead to paralysis now depends primarily on the regressive pull exerted by a latent illness" (pp. 166–167). Whether or not Martha is a latent schizophrenic, as she occasionally wonders (e.g., FG, p. 310), she is undeniably characterized by regressive tendencies. Her prolonged adolescence is a study in what Erikson calls "identity confusion," the inability to organize conflicting self-images around an integrating core. As Martha laments, "Why is it I listen for the echoes of other people in my voice and what I do all the time? The fact is, I'm not a person at all, I'm nothing yet—perhaps I never will be" (RS, p. 260).

The typical adolescent is characterized by his inability to choose among the various roles a beckoning society offers him. In a sense he is reviving the conflicts of his Oedipal phase, when his imagination ranged freely until it was balked by biology. But "where [the individual] regress[es] below the Oedipal crisis to a total crisis of trust, the choice of a self-defeating role often remains the only acceptable form of initiative" (Identity, p. 184). Martha is too insecure to rebel. She may dislike the available models, but her history is a consecutive account of adaptation to one proffered role after another. She is successively Matty the clown, Martha the young suburban wife and mother, and Comrade Matty. "There was nothing more paradoxical about her situation than that, while she insisted on being unique, individual, and altogether apart from any other person, she could be comforted . . . only by remarks like 'Everybody feels this' or 'It is natural to feel that' " (PM, p. 23).

Since the first volume of Children of Violence appeared in 1952, critics have persistently read the series as a critique of moribund society, hearing only the Martha who chafes at the restraints imposed by a colonial culture, which relegates women and blacks to mere functional identities. This Martha is indeed verbal: she rejects the models incarnate in the Dutch housewife Mrs. Van Rensberg and her own alienated mother, in the civil service wives whose husbands run the Left Book Club, and the black women whose fecundity is a reproach to their emancipated white sisters. But while Martha maintains that "her mind turned towards the heroines she had been offered, and discarded them" (MQ, p. 10), while she wonders "if . . . one had decided to be neither one nor the other, what could one be but fierce and unhappy and determined?" (MQ, p. 117), events give her protest a hollow ring. She grasps the lure of a fixed identity, however uncongenial she may find it, envying Joss his sense of vocation (MQ, p. 49), Alice her pregnancy (PM, p. 91), the native women their "wholeness" (PM, p. 19). After her marriage Martha finds "she had adapted herself so well to this life; some instinct to conform and comply had dictated that she must quell her loathing, as at entering a trap . . . She was instinctively compliant, enthusiastic, and took every step into bondage with affectionate applause for Douglas" (PM, p. 250).[13]

With physical maturity, Martha's "total crisis of trust" is revived most persistently in her repeated failure to achieve mutual love; she lacks that "firm self-delineation" (*Identity*, p. 167) which is the prior condition of true intimacy.

Adolescent love is "to a considerable extent . . . an attempt to arrive at a definition of one's identity by projecting one's diffused self-image on another and by seeing it thus reflected" (p. 132). Martha, learning that Douglas Knowell reads the liberal newspaper she takes, falls in love with him. "The shock of finding a fellow spirit was so exquisite that she could not hurry fast enough to the next confirmation of it . . . Not to tell him *everything* would have been a betrayal of their relationship; she felt as if she had known him forever" (MQ, pp. 217–218). Martha is so in love with the self she sees mirrored in Douglas, she does not even see him. When by chance she does, she quickly readjusts unpleasant facts:

> The round, rather low forehead struck her unpleasantly—there was something mean about it, something commonplace; the shallow dry lines across it affected her; as for his hands, they were large and clumsy, rather red, heavily freckled, and covered with hair. Soon she averted her eyes from his hands, she did not see them; she did not see his forehead, with those unaccountably unpleasant lines, like the lines of worry on an elderly face. She saw his eyes, the *approving* and warm blue eyes. *She had never known* this easy warm friendliness with anyone before; *she could say* what she liked; *she felt* altogether *approved*, and *she expanded* in it delightedly, and *her manner* lost its half-timid aggressiveness. (MQ, p. 218)

The words I have italicized further illustrate Martha's narcissism. Douglas does not exist, except in relation to her.

Even before she meets Douglas, Martha has fallen in love with another projection of herself, not her twin but her social conscience. When she meets

Adolph King, she has to struggle against a feeling of dislike, but she allows him to become her first lover because he is a Jew. Again, she sees not him but "Stella's approving nod, and Andrew smiling at her" (MQ, p. 173) as she shakes his hand in defiance of Sports Club anti-semitism. She feels "very sorry for him, in an impatient, contemptuous way," not recognizing that "this attitude was at bottom a sort of *noblesse oblige*" (MQ, p. 179). Some aspect of herself is in the balance, as she forces herself to ignore the "unpleasant and cowardly" person in order "to fight the world on his behalf—or at least her world" (MQ, p. 181). Martha must prove her liberalism, must defy "her world," must therefore go to bed with Adolph King, although she knows "that this man's body was wrong for her, that she was having her first love affair with a man she was not the slightest in love with" (MQ, p. 184). Years later, with another man, she is still not sure it is he she loves or the Russian revolution they both support (PM, p. 301).

If Douglas is her alter ego and Adolph her social conscience, Anton Hesse is Martha's mentor and protector. Again she willfully ignores his failings because "the need in her to admire and be instructed was so great" (RS, p. 155). "When I'm with him I feel safe" (RS, p. 91), she thinks; "contrary to what her instincts [tell] her about Anton" she has a feeling of "trust and relief . . . as if Anton's words built a pillar on which she could support herself" (RS, p. 122). Martha's infantile needs are consistently revealed in the orality of her love relationships. She decides to marry Anton "as if her whole being had concentrated itself into a movement of taking in and absorbing, as if she were swallowing something whole and hurrying on" (RS, p. 175).

For many adolescents intimacy is a threat. Lacking a firmly delineated sense of self, they see any love relationship as "an impersonal fusion amounting to a loss of identity" (*Identity*, p. 167), which Laing calls "engulfment." "The individual experiences himself as a man who is only saving himself from drowning by the most constant, strenuous, desperate activity" (*The Divided Self*, p. 44). But Martha, far from fearing fusion, longs for it. She "demand[s] nothing less than that the quintessence of all experience, all love, all beauty, should explode suddenly in a drenching, saturating moment of illumination" which will subsume her own partial identity and render "the man himself . . . positively irrelevant" (MQ, p. 184).

Most adolescents make the transition from the essentially private accretion of partial identities in childhood to the "subjective sense of an invigorating sameness and continuity" (*Identity*, p. 19) which enables them to move beyond identity to adult responsibility by choosing an ideology to which they can pledge fidelity (pp. 133–134). But Martha does not choose Communism for the ideals it embodies. It is not, for her, a rite of passage to social maturity and the assumption of responsibility for future generations. It is simply another of the larger identities in which she attempts to incorporate and define herself, and "she was conscious that the moment she left the group she felt as let down as if a physical support had been removed" (RS, p. 18). Any group would serve Martha's needs; she envies the airmen sitting near her in a restaurant, "possessed by an old feeling that she was being shut out of some warmth, some beautiful kind of friendship" (p. 112), and the Socialists she observes at a meeting, "feeling her old pain, that she was excluded from some good, some warmth, that she had never known" (p. 167).

In one encounter after another, vocational, sexual, or political, Martha reveals her fundamental modal orientation—"to get what is given"—and her doomed nostalgia for a lost paradise of symbiotic fusion. But we cannot understand Martha's development simply by studying her pathology. As Erikson reminds us, psychosocial strength . . . depends on a total process which regulates individual life cycles, the sequence of generations, and the structure of society simultaneously" (*Identity,* p. 141). And if the infant's first experience of mutuality is with a nurturing mother, it is important to remember that the mother who is the infant's first experience of a world outside himself "is not only a parturient creature but also a member of a family and society. She, in turn, must feel a certain wholesome relation between her biological role and the values of her community. Only thus can she communicate to the baby, in the unmistakable language of somatic interchange, that the baby may trust her, the world, and—himself. Only a relatively 'whole' society can vouchsafe to the infant, through the mother, an inner conviction that all the diffuse somatic experiences and all the confusing social cues of early life can be accommodated in a sense of continuity and sameness which gradually unites the inner and outer world" (p. 82). Turning from Martha to May Quest, we can better understand Martha's pathology, and, more significantly, begin to see that her arrested development is endemic. Martha's first contact with society is through her mother, who is both its representative and its victim. Looking at May Quest, we see how doomed is Martha's quest for social confirmation of her developing sense of identity.

3. MARTHA AND THE UNCONGENIAL SOCIETY

"Time, dear time, had brought her here, to lie on this bed, a small girl, inwardly weeping Mama, Mama, why are you so cold, so unkind?" (FG, p. 210). So Martha, at 35, reveals to herself and to us the underlying sense of rejection which has warped her development. Hers is the familiar history of the unwanted child, the girl who was born when a boy was hoped for, the daughter set aside in favor of the preferred son who was the second and last-born. Martha's memories of her childhood are few, and none of them is warm and sustaining. Overhearing her mother talking to her daughter Caroline, Martha wonders, "Do you suppose . . . that when I was little she talked to me like that? Is it possible she liked me enough?" (LL, p. 38).

The May Quest whom Martha remembers and against whom she rebelled was strong-willed, dominating her husband and daughter, cowing the neighbors with aggressive gentility. Enviously, Martha "could only think that Mrs. Quest had spent a free, energetic youth, had 'lived her own life'—she had used the phrase herself long before it was proper for middle-class daughters to do so—and had, accordingly, quarreled with her father. She had not married until very late" (PM, p. 96). Martha, who watches the adolescent metamorphoses of her own body with helpless loathing, remembers her mother's "white and beautiful hands" (PM, p. 94), her "heavy knot of hair . . . glistening gold where the light touched it from two candle flames which floated steadily above the long white transparent candles" (PM, p. 96) on the piano she had brought from England and on which she exquisitely played Chopin. A beautiful, a powerful, above all a self-confident woman, whom time and poverty reduced to "a rather tired but decided matron, with ambitious plans for her children" (MQ, p. 4).

This mother rejected Martha, who in turn rejects her, resolutely turning away from moments of insight into the long and gradual disappointment that living with a sick and shiftless husband on a poor farm on the high veld has made of Mrs. Quest's once promising life. For Martha pity is "contaminated" (PM, p. 261). It weakens her in her continuous battle to free herself from her mother's domination and from her need for that love her mother has denied her.

But if pity is Martha's "enemy" (FG, p. 222), it—or its stronger relation, compassion—is Lessing's mode of portraiture. Gradually through the five volumes that comprise *Children of Violence* she delineates a May Quest who is more vulnerable than Martha supposes, whose adult imperiousness is a mask assumed to hide the face of "a little girl deprived of something she badly wanted" (PM, p. 262).

In *Martha Quest,* Mrs. Quest is seen principally through Martha's eyes, from which perspective she seems both self-confident and domineering. Only briefly does the point of view shift (Part I, chapter 3) to Mrs. Quest's, when we overhear her concern that Martha is sacrificing her future to a lack of present ambition. This modified interior monologue only confirms the image of Mrs. Quest which Martha has begun to assemble for the reader: she is "angry," "peevish," bitter, self-justifying, blaming Martha and her husband for "the hard and disappointing life she had led since she came to the colony." There is something repellant about her "broad square, rather masculine face" with its calculated look of "patient regret," the weapon with which she knowingly overpowers her weak husband and helpless young daughter.

But in *A Proper Marriage* her face is "wistful" and "soft" as she dreams of Martha's unborn child as "the person her own two children had obstinately refused to become" (PM, p. 107). Her dreams of the child's future are impertinent and meddlesome, as Mr. Quest reminds her, but they arise from her need, from her "lonely unassuaged heart that was aching now with its emptiness" (PM, 108). Viewing Mrs. Quest without Martha's assistance, we begin to wonder whether her manner is an accurate translation of her self. It becomes increasingly more difficult to accept Martha's reading of her mother as Lessing gives us increasingly more frequent glimpses of "the small girl" (PM, pp. 110, 261–262) at the core of May Quest.

Martha envies her mother her youth. Knowing her own vulnerability, she compares her weakness to Mrs. Quest's strength: "she saw her mother . . . confronting . . . the Victorian father, the patriarchal father, with rebellion" (PM, p. 94). But Mrs. Quest "knew, when she put her hair up, deciding that she would *not* be a Victorian young lady, but must fight her stern father so that she could be a nurse (which no real lady was, in spite of Florence Nightingale) that her childhood had lacked something which she craved" (LL, p. 62).

Like Martha, Mrs. Quest has been deprived of the nurturing love of her mother. Like Martha's, this deprivation is revealed in her adult orality, her craving for sweets (PM, p. 258) and cigarettes (LL, p. 67), the regret which uncannily duplicates Martha's that "she, whose every instinct was for warm participation, was never allowed to be present" when "somewhere else people danced all night" (LL, p. 71). The aging Mrs. Quest has a dream in which:

her mother, reaching down from a high place which Mrs. Quest knew was heaven, handed her three red roses. . . . The beautiful young woman had leaned down, smiling, from heaven, and handed the daughter she had scarcely known three red roses, fresh with bright water. Mrs. Quest, weeping with joy, her heart opening to her beautiful mother, had looked down and seen that in her hand the roses had turned into—a medicine bottle. . . . She wept at the cruelty of the dream. Medicine bottles, yes; that was her life, given her by a cruel and mocking mother. (LL, pp. 61–63)

Martha imagines that her mother had been beautiful; Mrs. Quest knows that *her* mother was. But her dream of the red roses brings her finally to the realization that her mother had been "unkind," self-centered, and vain, rejecting the little girl everyone had called plain (FG, p. 239). Defined by that cruelty, Mrs. Quest drew up "an unloved little girl," the nurse who accepted "handsome Captain Quest" with gratitude and thereafter "had no choice but to sacrifice herself" (FG, p. 241).

For Martha, fighting to overcome her own deprivation and struggling against the enemy, pity, her mother must be "summed up" and even dismissed "by the insensitivity, the hideousness" of her salmon-pink sweater (LL, p. 75). But Mrs. Quest dreams that

The scent of roses came in through the window, and she smiled. This time they remained in her hand—three crimson roses. That brutal woman, her beautiful mother, remained invisible in her dangerous heaven. . . . Mrs. Quest had become her own comforter, her own solace. Having given birth to herself, she cradled Mrs. Quest, a small frightened girl, who lay in tender arms against a breast covered in the comfort of bright salmon-pink, home-knitted wool. (LL, pp. 77–78)[1]

As long as Mrs. Quest is reliving her own birth trauma, she is incapable of mothering Martha. Her mother's sins blight generations. Martha's "Mama, Mama, why are you so cold, so unkind" both echoes her mother's tears and reminds her of her own daughter Caroline:

White shoes; small white shoes, a child's; a small girl with a pink dress and shining black curls. She turned her face towards Martha, a small, rather sharp face, watchful. Her smile was strained. Martha reached towards the smile, saw it dissolve in tears: Martha heard herself crying. She wept, while a small girl wept with her, Mama, Mama, why are you so cold, so unkind, why did you never love me? (FG, p. 221)

Caught in the mesh of her own needs and fears, Martha sets Caroline free, refusing to repeat the mistakes she accuses her mother of. But what is to save Caroline from interpreting that gesture, in some future dream of her own, as Martha's abandoning her?

Martha is hounded by "the nightmare *repetition*" (PM, p. 77), a hydra-headed monster which would impede her growth on at least three fronts. As she vaguely senses, her personal psychological handicap repeats her mother's and threatens her daughter:

> My poor unfortunate brat, what had you done to deserve a mother like me? Well, there's no help for it, you'll just have to put up with it. . . . You and I are just victims, my poor child, you can't help it, I can't help it, my mother couldn't help it, and her mother . . ." (PM, p. 204)

But Lessing suggests that this pattern is part of another, related but larger. Martha is doomed to repetition by her sex. Although he has only "half her brains" (MQ, p. 26), her brother is sent away to school, while Martha is allowed, even encouraged, to stay on the farm, idly reading. Fired with ambition to become a writer, she is offered a minor job on the woman's page of the *Zambesia News* (MQ, p. 210); although she feels herself "capable of much more" (MQ, p. 95), she is advised to become an "efficient secretary" like the model Mrs. Buss. Her friends discount her first attempts to become politically conscious, confident that "Douggie'll put some sense into her head. You can't be a Red if you're married to a civil servant" (PM, p. 20).

Thus it is not only Martha's regressive longing for the security and love she was denied in her infancy that determines her characteristic passivity, but a set of social expectations which confirm, almost institutionalize, her dominant oral modality. Dressed to attract men, vocationally restricted to reproducing their thoughts in shorthand, rewarded by their gifts of chocolate and expensive dinners, and presumably fulfilled by accepting one's name and bearing his child, she is expected, in short, to be graciously incorporative. Her individual pathology is reinforced by her culture and in turn makes her its willing victim. Martha alternately recoils from the roles society offers her and yields to their seduction. After her marriage to Douglas, she reflects that while "she had been sucked into the pattern, with part of herself she connived at it" (PM, p. 251).

Individual pathology and sexual type casting work together to create impediments to Martha's growth. But as hers is not merely a personal neurosis, so it is not only a woman's problem. She is not alone in her sense of entrapment. Discharged from the Army because of his ulcer, Douglas gloomily looks forward to a future with "nothing unexpected, nothing new from one year's end to the next. Holidays every five years or so, retirement, death" (PM, p. 223). And Donovan, who "should have been a dress designer" (MQ, p. 147), knows that "if one is raised in the colonies, then what can one do but go into statistics and wait for one's chief to retire!" (MQ, pp. 147–148). As Martha observes bitterly to Mr. Maynard, life in the colony is "like a— Victorian novel . . . It's all so boring, things happen the same way over and over again" (PM, p. 187).

Martha's nightmare repetition is Stephen Dedalus' definition of history:

"a nightmare from which I am trying to awake." And this is because Martha's society has no living history, but only a set of forms and patterns inherited from the past.

"Human strength," Erikson maintains, "depends on a total process which regulates at the same time the sequence of generations and the structure of society. . . . To use, once more, hope as an example: the emergence of this vital quality can be seen as defined by three coordinates: the relation of the mother's motherhood to her own past childhood; the mother-child relation itself; and the relation of both to institutions providing faith in procreation" (*Insight and Responsibility*, p. 152). As we have seen, Mrs. Quest's own childhood deprivations, her painful isolation from a vain and selfish mother, provide her no model for maternity. The psychic damage she has sustained precludes any nourishing relationship to her children. Her willful Anglicism and snobbishness reveal, however, that there is more than individual pathology at the root of her inability to establish a maternal relationship to Martha. Like her husband, she is a "dream-locked figure" (MQ, p. 24), living the outmoded patterns of Victorian England which, although they were personally painful, were at least comprehensible to her.

Advising his engaged daughter not to have children, Mr. Quest reminds Martha that "we didn't mean to have you, the doctor said we were neither of us in a fit state. . . . We were both having severe nervous breakdowns, due to the Great Unmentionable" (MQ, p. 239), and Martha muses, "that man and that woman, when they conceived me, one was in shell-shock from the war, and the other in a breakdown from nursing its wounded. She, Martha, was as much a child of the 1914–1918 war as she was of Alfred Quest, May Quest" (LL, p. 196). Like most self-analyses, these statements of the problem are only partially correct. The "double nervous breakdown" that engendered Martha was not so much the result of shell-shock and exhaustion as a metaphor for the loss of the old order. *Children of Violence* is not centrally concerned with the effect of the First World War on social history; Martha, the child of that war, not her father its victim, is its protagonist. But the process that Ford Madox Ford anatomizes in *Parades End* is implicit in the characters of Mr. and Mrs. Quest.

They cannot articulate what it is about the world they live in which baffles them. They fulminate imprecisely about "the international ring of Jews who controlled the world" or "lazy kaffirs" or Hitler who "was no gentleman" (MQ, p. 26). Retreating from what they cannot comprehend, they take refuge in the remembered world that ordered their youth. Mr. Quest remembers the war itself with "an undercurrent of burning regret. Then he had been alive. 'The comradeship,' he would exclaim, 'the comradeship! I've never experienced that since!' " (PM, p. 69). And Mrs. Quest clings to a pattern of gentility, leaving visiting cards on her uncomprehending Dutch neighbors (MQ, p. 14) and superimposing a Chopin nocturne on the night noises of the African bush (PM, p. 96).

Mr. Quest senses that he lost not only his health but "something more important than health" in the war (MQ, p. 20). What he and all of us lost was the "reasonably coherent world" (*Identity,* p. 106) which Erikson posits as the necessary foundation of the faith mothers transmit to their children, a world Thomas Stern sums up for Martha in his story of the elm tree:

> It was once like this: a child was born in a house that had a tree outside it. It was an elm tree. His grandfather had planted it. The child grew up while the tree shed its leaves and grew them again. He quarrelled with his father, but afterwards lay under the elm tree and felt at peace. He slept with his first girl under the elm tree, and their baby was put to sleep under the elm tree, and when his wife died she was buried under the elm tree, and as an old man, he stood at his gate and looked at the tree, and thought: That tree has been with me all my life. (LL, p. 117)

Throughout her youth, Martha is drawn to anachronistic patterns of coherence, ethnic subcultures still shaded by an elm tree. She envies Joss Cohen his Jewishness, the identity he assumes with his shopkeeper's black coat (MQ, p. 49), and the natives who live "according to their instincts" (PM, p. 63), but even more appealing are the Dutch settlers who have established "a close-knit, isolated community" and whose speech "had the rich cadences of a living religion" (MQ, p. 46).

Above all, Martha like her parents looks to England for the reasonable coherence of established tradition. Like them she resonates with "half-buried, half-childish, myth-bred emotions" to the words "Piccadilly Circus, Eros, Hub, Centre, London, England" (FG, p. 22). The first four volumes of *Children of Violence* throb to a gathering momentum of Martha's desire to go to England: "I am going to the sea, oh, soon, soon, because I shall go crazy soon if I can't reach the sea" (LL, p. 220), and when she finally arrives, she feels she has come "home" (FG, p. 16).

At first she wanders around London anonymously, feeling "what she had been before she had left 'home' to come 'home' . . . a taste or flavour of existence without a name" (FG, p. 16). As in Zambesia, she observes but feels excluded from the solidarity and cohesion of the subcultures represented by Stella and the dockers or Iris and Jimmy in their cafe. But when she first enters Mark Coldridge's house, she "knew that for the first time in her life she was in a setting where, if she chose to stay, there would be no doubt at all of how she ought to behave, to dress" (FG, p. 85). The house in Bloomsbury was

> of a piece, a totality: yet no one could set out to create a house like it. It had grown

like this, after being furnished by Mark's grandmother at the end of the last century by what Martha would have called when she first came 'antiques' . . . Every object, surface, chair, piece of material, or stuff or paper had—solidity. Strength. Nothing could crack, fray, fall apart . . . The curtains had a weight in your hands. The carpet and the rugs lay thick on the boards of the floor which were beautiful enough to lie bare, if there were not so many rugs and carpets. Nothing in this house believed in the possibility of destruction. Imagine being brought up in such a house, to be the child of it. (FG, p. 102)

In the last awed whisper speaks the child of May and Albert Quest who has found in Radlett Street, Bloomsbury, the embodiment of that old-fashioned "quality" that stands for England, virtue, meaning, and order.

That England is also housed with Mary and Harold Butts, Mark Coldridge's old nanny and her gardener husband who have retired to the country. "That house, in its old village, with its quiet people, was England, as one had always imagined it. . . . In a little cottage bedroom that smelled all through the summer of the flowers Harold Butts grew, Martha lay and thought, Yes this is England, this was what they meant when they said England. This is what my father meant" (FG, p. 171).

"Except that ten miles away was a war place where new atomic weapons were being developed, in secret; and forty miles away in another direction was a factory for the manufacture of gasses and poisons for use in war" (FG, p. 171). And Martha discovers soon after she moves into Mark's house that it "was in a dreadful state beneath its surface of order" (FG, p. 111). Its "white surfaces" are merely a façade "over a structure attacked by war and damp" (FG, p. 288).

The Buttses, like the Dutch colony in Zambesia, are an anachronism. As Thomas knows, "everything's changed . . . The elm tree and safety's finished" (LL, p. 168). Thomas Stern, whose peasant roots are under an elm tree in Sochaczen, Poland, is "the norm now. . . . My family's all dead and I'm in exile. And my wife's family are dead and she's an exile" (LL, p. 168). A world without reasonable coherence can drive you mad, as it does Thomas. Or you can, as Mark does, duplicating May and Albert Quest, assert that previous patterns of coherence are still viable. The story of Colin Coldridge is a parable of the imperfections of Mark's method of coping with reality.

Colin, Mark's brother, is a nuclear physicist. When the man he works with is accused of spying for the Russians, Colin comes under suspicion as well. Mark at first treats it as a joke because "of course, if one lived in such houses, filled with such furniture, knowing 'everybody' in England, then spying was—a joke. Or rather, the idea that they could be suspected of it" (FG, p. 104). But it is no joke, as Mark discovers when Colin defects to the Soviet Union. Mark suddenly discovers that the old categories of *noblesse oblige* and gentlemanliness are inadequate to the realities of espionage and counterespionage, that England, like any other country, "employs spies . . . taps telephones, opens letters, and keeps dossiers on its citizens" (FG, p. 173). When he discovers that he is under suspicion too, and that an old friend of the family has used the customary forms of friendship to spy on him, Mark "has a nervous breakdown" (FG, p. 173), an echo of the double nervous breakdown Martha's parents suffered when the war shattered the old order for them.

Mark resembles the senior Quests not only in his nervous breakdown, but in his incapacity as a parent. Martha, who has suffered from her parents' attempts to impose outmoded ideas of order on her reality, questions Mark's decision to send his son Francis to a public school. "They have some kind of a strength," he answers, "I haven't got it. I want him to have it. . . . Oh I dare say it's a kind of narrowness. They're blinkered. If you like" (FG, p. 121). But it isn't a question of what Martha likes, it's a question of facts. That "strength" represented for Mark by public schools, family tradition, and gentlemanliness, is the strength of blind Samson. Mary and Harold Butts, who have it, do not see "the death factories so close to them" (FG, p. 171). Mark, who is "bogged down" (FG, p. 431) in his and England's past, can offer nothing of value to Francis, who is forced instead into "an extraordinary love for his father—all protective, as if Mark were his son. He seemed concerned, often, that his father should be saved from the nasty realities of life" (FG, p. 432).[2]

It is not the collapse of the old order that impedes Martha's growth to self-definition, however, so much as its lingering potency. Its appeal to her is always associated with water imagery; yearning for the reasonable coherence that no longer shapes society is another of Martha's regressions, another capitulation to lying nostalgia, as she comes increasingly to acknowledge. Martha dreams of England as " 'that country' . . . pale, misted, flat; gulls cried like children around violet-colored shores. She stood on coloured chalky rocks with a bitter sea washing around her feet and the smell of salt was strong in her nostrils" and the dream has "the peculiarly nostalgic quality which she distrusted so much, and yet was so dangerously attractive to her" (RS, p. 84).

But the old order is more than a focus for Martha's oceanic longings. As another of her dreams makes clear, it has a sinister menace independent of any role it may play in her private psychological drama. Martha has a dream of the past as "an immense lizard, an extinct saurian that had been imprisoned a thousand ages ago in the rock." But—and this gives the dream its nightmarish quality—the monster is not dead, "and it will take centuries more to die." The lizard stares at Martha with its ancient eye, and the horror to her is that it is "too old even to see" her (RS, p. 85).

The menace of the old order is its capacity to blind us to present reality. If you persist in seeing an elm tree that isn't there, you can't see the real forest.

Shortly before she leaves for England, Martha visits her parents (LL, Part IV, chapter 2). Her father's chronic invalidism has become his terminal illness; Martha's six-year old daughter, who does not know Martha is her mother and must not be told, is alone with him in his room, and Martha is in the living room, contemplating a set of "enormous black keys such as no one used these days" which her mother has assembled for her. These keys from Mrs. Quest's past are her farewell gift to her daughter, and they symbolize for Martha the "preposterousness" of the entire situation of her parents' house.

What is preposterous is the looming chasm between fact and fiction, between the "surface of sense, of civilized life" and "a situation for which there were no precedents." Confronted with the fact that her daughter has abandoned her child "without the wailing, the weeping, the wringing of the hands that make it, almost, an act within nature (as the writers of Victorian melodrama understood very well)," Mrs. Quest invents the consoling fiction that Martha is Caroline's Auntie Matty. Confronted with a "sick old man who scarcely knew what he was doing," Mrs. Quest comforts herself with the cliché that "it's nice for the poor little girl to get to know her grandfather while she has the chance." Confronted with a daughter who faces an uncharted future without luggage, Mrs. Quest presents her with "all the keys she had ever had in her life." Confronted by a situation for which there are no precedents, Mrs. Quest blindly alters the situation to fit the precedents she has—a set of keys, "black, rusty, jutting, awkward."

In the plot Martha gives Mark for his space-fiction novel, the fabled Utopian city is destroyed not by earthquake or a meteor from outer space, but by the shadow city which grows up around it, emulating its form but lacking its organic inner order.

The old order is Eliot's "shape without form, shade without colour, / Paralysed force, gesture without motion." At best it is irrelevant. At worst, it stifles growth by glossing over the facts which—however disorderly—are the only possible basis for realistic action, as Mrs. Quest's fictions expose Caroline to the "horror" of a dying man's existential agony but deny her any legitimate reaction to it.

Martha's quest for identity is chartless. She has neither the compass of infantile security nor the map of living institutions by which to define and affirm her emerging self. Indeed her only hope lies in her daring to strip herself of the malevolent vestiges of her past, to begin her search for herself with "a radical search for the rock-bottom" which is Erikson's term for the essential core of individual reality which is "the only firm foundation for . . . progression" (*Identity*, p. 212).

Her task is twofold. Acknowledging that her family provided her no sustaining basis for growth, she must identify the actual sources of her unique personhood. And refusing to accept the dead forms of a remembered social order, she must define her culture as it is, before she can assume her place in it.

4. MARTHA AND HER METAPHORS:
FROM THE SHELL TO THE GREAT BELL OF SPACE

The derelict car that transports the Quests from their farm to the nearby town has a broken gas gauge. So the resourceful Mr. Quest, who has already patched the cracked radiator with eggs, devises a method of his own for determining how much gas is in the tank. If it is seven miles from the house to the station, then half-way there the tank should be half full of gas. In fact it is only five and three-quarter miles to the station. Characteristically, Mr. Quest has imposed a fictional seven miles on the real five and three-quarters, "for to have a house in the dead centre of a magically determined circle offers satisfaction beyond all riches, and even power." But, as Martha critically reflects, "a poetical seven miles is one thing, and to check one's petrol gauge by it another" (MQ, p. 33).

Martha, however, has grown up to the accompaniment of her parents' time-locked "litanies of suffering" and "the words 'no man's land,' 'star shells,' 'Boche,' touched off in her images like those of poetry" (p. 25). But unlike her parents, who choose to live in a fictional world, Martha "was afraid because of the power of these words, which affected her so strongly, who had nothing to do with what they stood for" (p. 25). Determined not to run out of gas halfway to her destination, Martha tries to reject poetry in favor of fact. But finding facts is not easy in a culture that denies or distorts them to fit the shapelier patterns of fiction.

Martha's quest for identity is at least in part a literary problem. She must turn her back on the stale conventions of the past and create new ones to represent things as they are. She must find images for herself and the world she lives in to replace the hyperboles of her parents.

Erikson's clinical experience leads him to assert that when patients plummet to the rock-bottom, the bare and essential core of selfhood, they discover there an imperative to "redelineate" themselves (*Identity*, p. 213). This aesthetic metaphor is a particularly apt one for Martha, whose childhood illumination predicted her necessary rebirth in plastic terms: "What was demanded of her was that she should accept something quite different . . . as if it were a necessity, which she must bring herself to accept, that she should allow herself to dissolve and be formed by that necessity" (MQ, p. 53). Moreover, as Erikson has noted, redelineation is associated with an individual's "quasideliberate surrender to the pull of regression" (*Identity*, p. 212). Martha "dissolves," a characteristically oral and regressive activity for her, before she can "be formed." Her creative efforts to find accurate images for herself and the world she lives in are continually impeded by her dominant orality. While she rejects the dead metaphors bequeathed her by her heritage, she is persistently drawn to images which reinforce her pathology.

Martha initially thinks of herself as a "soft, shell-less creature" (PM, p. 94). Without examining that metaphor, she operates in terms of it, beginning her quest for identity by moving from one shell to another, trying to find one that will fit, concluding that none does. But while Martha is working with one implication of her metaphor—the problem of finding a shell—Lessing allows another to reverberate. The soft, shell-less creature evokes correlative images of helplessness and vulnerability, of babyhood. Martha tries to revise her self-image without understanding it, but we evaluate her progress toward identity according to the proximity of successive images to this first one, according to how far Martha has moved beyond infancy.

The first shell Martha tries on is clothing. Her self-image is initially formed by the dresses her mother chooses for her, but they "looked ugly, even obscene, for her breasts were well grown, and the yokes emphasized them, showing flattened bulges under the tight band of material; and the straight falling line of the skirt was spoiled by her full hips" (MQ, p. 16). The vital shape of Martha's adolescent body defies her mother's definition of propriety, as later it defies Donovan's ideas of slim-hipped elegance. To wear the dresses he designs, Martha must again "strain" (p. 141) her image of herself to fit. Her first attempt to define herself is to reject the "false images" (p. 141) of her self created by the clothes others have chosen for her.

As clothes have distorted her real shape, so they also seem to Martha to have the power to express her real self.[1] She sees a dress in a shop window which is "made to clothe the person she knew herself to be" (p. 141). Too timid to wear the dress and flaunt her self at the Sports Club, she buys it and puts it away in a corner of her closet. Years later she wears it to please Thomas Stern, only to discover that it too has become another false statement. What Martha realizes, sitting uncomfortably in her beautiful dress, is that it is not enough to express the shape and style of her body with the clothes she wears. The blue dress is true to the womanly body it clothes. But that body itself inaccurately reflects Martha's sense of herself. A beautiful woman is a "painted shell" (RS, p. 114) whose appearance has nothing to say of her hopes and fears and needs. Martha begins to think of her appearance, her public self, as a "shell of substance" (LL, p. 15). Somewhere inside is the real Martha, who, she has learned, will not be expressed by any "shell for living in" (PM, p. 65).

Martha pragmatically accepts the protection of various shells, however ill-fitting they may be. She adopts the role of suburban housewife, knowing that "three parts of herself stood on one side, idle, waiting to be called into action" (p. 250). She endures years of compliance, because "they had all been a lie against her real nature, and therefore they had not existed" (p. 307). The life styles she adopts are "bastions of defense" (p. 94), behind which the essential Martha shelters while she gropes for a knowledge of her real dimensions. But what Martha sees as progress, Lessing implies, is merely a sequence of permutations of her infantile self-image. Martha thinks she has asserted her identity in opposition to the identifications others have made of her. In fact, as long as she thinks of that identity, that self, as living inside a shell, she remains a soft shell-less infant whose relation to others is essentially passive and dependent.

Martha, when she is pregnant, begins to think of her true, inner self as a lighthouse. During labor she thinks of pain as an ocean that threatens to "engulf" her; the "small lit place in her brain" (p. 144) which is her self fights the dehumanizing pain of her contractions. This kind of thinking is a normal enough instance of self-induced anesthesia, but Martha's detachment from her body becomes as characteristic a mode of self-identification as her detachment from the costumes and roles that would falsely identify her.

Martha dissociates her self from her body because it would "implicate" her (p. 127) in the confining patterns she senses she must resist. It is Martha's body that feels, not only the pangs of labor, but "a slow, warm, heavy longing" to have a second child, which would condemn her to "live in the pattern till she died" (p. 251). Martha's body is in collusion with at least one of the shells which Martha, who prefers to think of herself as a free spirit, finds constricting. Her body, by its committment to "the cycle of procreation" (p. 152), would lock Martha into the nightmare repetition and limit her identity to that of the "petty-bourgeois colonial" (p. 131) that she scorns.

Further, as the lighthouse image suggests, Martha separates her self from her body at least in part as a defense against her own regressive tendencies. Whenever Martha becomes confused by the "half a dozen entirely different people" who inhabit her body, she reacts with "a strong impulse of longing: anonymous, impersonal, formless, like water." Images of water in *Children of Violence* always alert us to Martha's temptation to give up the quest for identity, to merge herself into an established role that would relieve her of the difficult task of discovering who she uniquely is. In marrying Douglas Knowell and becoming a suburban matron, Martha is "completely swept away . . . gone on the tide." She longs to "lapse into" motherhood and domesticity "as into a sea and let everything go." Later she is "dissolved" into a love affair with Thomas Stern in which she becomes not who she is, but who he wants her to be. She has a sensation of "sinking" into "deep waters" (LL, p. 153).

Growth, as Erikson has observed, "is a process of increasing differentiation" (*Identity*, p. 23). It begins at birth, when we are ejected from the warm protective waters of the womb. And insofar as Martha keeps herself "above the dark blind sea," refusing to be "submerged" or "dragged back" by her yearning for absorption into the "community" (PM, p. 150) of wives and mothers, she has elected to grow. She rejects identification with that community in order to arrive at a sense of her own identity. So, too, she resists being "dissolved so absolutely" (LL, p. 100) in her affair with Thomas. "When what she had been waiting for happened at last," when she was "suck[ed] into an intensity of feeling" (p. 81) with a man, "she discovered that creature in her self whom she had cherished in patience, fighting and reluctant" (p. 100). Dissociating her self from her oceanic impulses, Martha becomes "a lighthouse of watchfulness." She is "a being totally on the defensive" (p. 14).[2]

On at least two fronts, dividing her self is a good defensive strategy for Martha. It enables her to gain some control over her own regressive tendencies, and it accurately evaluates the constricting partiality of the shells and patterns that society would impose on her as substitutes for identity. By identifying her body as just another shell, Martha puts all shells in their place. To the extent that she knows none can express her real shape, she is free to discover the dimensions of her true self. She finds it "necessary to strengthen, to polish, to set off the attractive Matty, the shell . . . this shell of substance, smooth brown flesh so pleasantly curved into the shape of young woman with smooth browny-gold hair" (pp. 14–15), because it will keep people from discovering and threatening the real Martha who lives somewhere "underneath these metamorphoses of style or shape" (pp. 13–14).

In one of her therapeutic sessions with Dr. Lamb in *The Four-Gated City*, Martha voices the fear that her sense of being divided may mean that she, like Lynda, is mad. But when she tells him she feels like two people, only one of whom—the watcher—is "real," his response is an "affable" nod (FG, p. 227). He repeatedly reassures her, "I do promise you, you can take my word for it, you're not a schizophrenic" (p. 310). Martha's schizoid defensive posture does not incapacitate her in her relations with the world. It may be the most appropriate posture for living in a world deluded by its fictions. As Laing observes, complete "adaptation to a dysfunctional society may be very dangerous."[3] By preserving a sense of her self as distinct from her false self, her shell, Martha holds herself aloof from that danger.

The real danger to Martha in thinking of herself as divided is that it perpetuates her infantile dependence and passivity. Inside her protective shell Martha is freed from the necessity to establish vigorous and realistic contact with the world around her. But that freedom, paradoxically, impedes her progress on the road to self-knowledge. Encapsulated in her shell, Martha is cut off from the community around her which, Erikson contends, is the confirming context of an achieved sense of personal identity.

"To be a person, identical with oneself, presupposes a basic trust in one's origins," Erikson asserts (*Insight and Responsibility*, p. 95). Martha's biological parents have betrayed her trust. Her mother, by forcing Martha's body into standard school-girl frocks, has prevented her from acquiring the most fundamental sense of her own bodiliness. By imposing their ideas of order on the African environment, the senior Quests and their fellow colonizers have camouflaged Martha's cultural origins as well. Seeing herself as she is involves for Martha seeing her society as it really is. She must know her origins in order to trust them.

The town where she goes to work when she leaves her parents' farm is as adolescent and unformed as Martha herself, "at a crossroads in its growth: half a modern city, half a pioneers' achievement" (PM, p. 4). On top of this chaos, the town planners create order by "laying a ruler neatly over a map which represented a patch of unused veld, causing a pattern of streets to come into existence which crossed each other regularly at right angles. Everything was straight, orderly, unproblematical" (p. 246) and, to Martha, "dismaying and distasteful" (p. 255) because it is false to what it presumes to order.

Like the town planners, Mr. and Mrs. Quest impose a grid of fictions on the scrubby reality of their few high-veld acres. Even as a girl, Martha wonders "why . . . the family [has] always given large-sounding names to things ordinary and even shabby" (MQ, p. 23). She has sensed all along that the farm she grows up on bears no relation to "the literature that was her tradition" in which "the word *farm* evokes an image of something orderly, compact, cultivated; a neat farmhouse in a pattern of fields" (p. 2).

Underneath the imposed forms of the Victorian novel (PM, p. 187), the district where Martha grows up is "divided into several separate communities, who shared nothing but Christian names, cards at Christmas, and a member of Parliament" (MQ, p. 45). To lament this lack of community, to long for the old order, as Martha does when she envies the Van Rensbergs their subculture, is to retreat from fact into the comfortable fictions of the senior Quests. Martha sees more clearly when she accepts her fragmented society for what it is, in a passage whose language and rhythm ally it to that "illumination" which she regards as her "lodestone, even her conscience" :

She stood on the veranda of Socrates' store, and looked over the empty dusty space to the railway line, and thought of the different people who passed there; the natives, the nameless and swarming; the Afrikaans [sic], whose very name held the racy poetic quality of their vigorous origins; the British, with their innumerable subgroupings, held together only because they could say, 'this is a British country'—held together by the knowledge of ownership. And each group, community, clan, colour, strove and fought away from the other, in a sickness of dissolution; it was as if the principle of separateness was bred from the very soil, the sky, the driving sun; as if the inchoate vastness of the universe, always insistent in the enormous unshrouded skies, the enormous mountain-girt horizons, so that one might never, not for a moment, forget the inhuman, relentless struggle of soil and water and light, bred a fever of self-assertion in its children like a band of explorers lost in a desert, quarrelling in an ecstacy of fear over their direction, when nothing but a sober mutual trust could save them. Martha could feel the striving forces in her own substance: the effort of imagination needed to destroy the words *black, white, nation, race,* exhausted her, her head ached.   (MQ, p. 47)

So in London, years later, does Martha reflect that "this business of having to divide off, make boundaries—it was such a strain" (FG, p. 33). This desire to categorize is as much a Victorian legacy as the silver tea tray on the Quests' sideboard. The fact is that it is not up to Martha or any individual either to keep blacks and whites apart or to bring them together. As Martha finally realizes, "there was something in the human mind that separated, and divided . . . For the insight of knowledge she now held, of the nature of separation, of division . . . was clear and keen—she understood . . . understood *really* (but in a new way, was in the grip of a vision), how human beings could be separated so absolutely by a slight difference in the texture of their living that they could not talk to each other, must be wary, or enemies" (p. 79). Although that vision of reality is not articulated by Martha until she is middle-aged, it is the same vision she had as a girl of "each group, community, clan, colour" striving away from each other "in a sickness of dissolution . . . as if the principle of separateness was bred from the very soil."

The truth is neither pretty nor comfortable. Martha sees the dissolution as a sickness, just as earlier she had known that "what she had been waiting for like a revelation was a pain, not a happiness." Only fiction has happy endings, but we and Martha have sensed the menace of Mrs. Quest's happy fictions to Caroline, whose eyes as they meet Martha's have a premature "sharp almost cynical knowledge" (LL, p. 236) that her grandfather really is dying, that Martha really is her mother, and that grandma really is lying.

As long as Martha recoils, like her mother, from ugly reality, she will be a minor poet, unable to create a metaphor for her self. Her stature as a poet and her hope as a human being depend on her willigness to accept the pain that accompanies illumination. Her mature vision of reality is both painful and exultant: "This was the real truth of what went on not only here but everywhere: everything declined and frayed and came to pieces in one's hands . . . a mass of fragments, like a smashed mirror" (p. 337). Her growth to self-knowledge can be measured by her willingness to accept the analogous truth that she is herself "a mass of fragments" (p. 336).

Martha is not a true self housed in a false self. Such a binary configuration misrepresents the fact that Martha is "different selves" (MQ, p. 156), "half a dozen entirely different people" (p. 143) at the same time. Ironically, by preserving a sense of her self as divided between a central, unembodied true self and a system of false selves or public identities, Martha perpetuates the compartmentalization she inveighs against when she romantically contrasts the simple native women who live "according to their instincts" with women like herself who "think and disintegrate themselves into fragments" (PM, p. 63). Only by acknowledging the fragmented self she truly is can Martha move toward integration. She is able to create a metaphor for her self when she finds its analogue in the society that surrounds and contains her, when she redefines her origins and reinvests her basic trust.

When the Quests move to town, "Martha felt a sadness which she understood was shared by her father when he said, 'It's all very well . . . but I feel so damned *shut* in, with all these streets.' . . . Martha felt an exile, as he did. She did not know how much it had meant that her parents, at least, had been on the land. . . . Now she felt altogether cut off from her roots" (p. 128). Martha senses that her roots, her origins, are in her native Zambesia, not England, and of this time, not some vaguely remembered antebellum order. The "shells and surfaces of brick and concrete" (MQ, p. 230) which the city planners impose on the veld create order and comfort and prosperity, but Martha longs for "the veld she had been brought up on, the sere, empty, dry vleis, the scrubby little trees, the enormous burnt windy spaces of the high veld" (PM, p. 254). Whenever Martha capitulates to her parents' and their culture's rage for order, she betrays her basic trust in her origins. Whenever she substitutes "digging in a tame vegetable bed" (PM, p. 254) for walking on the veld, whenever she makes "the effort of imagination needed to destroy the words *black, white, nation, race*" which accurately reflect the Zambesia she lives in, she blurs her vision.

Contaminated by her parents' unfriendliness toward the facts, the young Martha looked at the veld that stretched away from her front porch and "refashioned that unused country to the scale of her imagination. There arose, glimmering whitely over the harsh scrub and the stunted trees, a noble city, set foursquare and colonnaded along its falling, flower-bordered terraces." In Martha's dream city, there are no divisions of race and color, but "forever excluded from the golden city because of their pettiness of vision and small understanding" (MQ, p. 11) are her parents and all the other inhabitants of the district. As a typist in a small colonial city, lying back on her bed "eating chocolate," she is still dreaming of an ideal city "where people altogether generous and warm exchanged generous emotions" (p. 120). And she is drawn to Communism because Jasmine and the other comrades share her Utopian vision of "an ideal town, clean, noble and beautiful, soaring up over the actual town" they live in, "which consisted . . . of sordid little shops and third-rate cafes" (RS, p. 27). Martha believes "she could have drawn a plan of that city, from the central market place to the four gates" (MQ, p. 11). As long as she imposes this imaginary blueprint over the world she really lives in, Martha is neither architect nor poet, but merely a city planner, willfully drawing grids over the fecund formlessness of reality.

Only when Mark Coldridge turns her dream into science fiction does Martha understand the dimensions of her task. "She had once sat under a tree and looked across the veld and imagined a city shining there in the scrub. An ideal city, full of fountains and flowers. Like Mark's city. Perhaps the same city: but both, after all, were imagined. What had that stretch of country looked like?" (FG, p. 206).

Martha's problem is that she forgets too easily. Returning to the farm for a weekend shortly after she has first left it to work for the Cohen brothers in town, she sees the veld "like an astonished stranger" (MQ, p. 230). Ruggedly asserting its independence of both the English order that Mr. and Mrs. Quest try to impose on it and the shimmering mirage of Martha's four-gated city, the African veld is "sere" and "empty." Here are no Wordsworthian daffodils but "dryness, barrenness, stunted growth, the colours that are fed from starved roots—thin browns and greys, dull greens and sad yellows—and all under a high, dry, empty sky" (PM, p. 254).

The aging Mrs. Quest dreams of the sea as her husband remembers the lush wetness of the English countryside. They have "had enough of mountains, peaks, rocks, dryness and the winds that shrank one's flesh till one felt all dried skin on old bones" (FG, p. 237). So in her immaturity would Martha return "to her old nurse, the sea," longing "to get off this high, dry place where my skin burns and where I can never lose the feeling of tension" (LL, p. 199).

But in wiser moments Martha acknowledges that "the thoughts of a planned and comfortable country, filled with prosperous villas in green and fruitful acres, was dismaying and distasteful" (PM, pp. 254–255). Her roots are in that vast, empty, barren land of Africa, an "enormous stretch of country lifted high, high, under a high pale-blue cloudswept sky" (LL, p. 159).[4]

But even as Martha acknowledges the ugliness and pain and fragmentation that characterize reality, even as she discards her own and her parents' fictitious images, she is betrayed by her pathology. Even as she turns her back to the sea and her thoughts from verdant England, she invests the veld with oceanic qualities. Increasingly the veld comes to mean space for Martha, space as container, space as amplitude, space—in short—as mother. On a drive across the veld, Martha gazes "with passionate curiosity" into the empty space and discovers there the answer to the fragmentation that frightens her:

> She saw Maisie, if there had not been a war: married to her first husband, producing a child, two children. . . . Soon she would have been a fat, middle-aged woman with reserves of lazy good nature, and spoiled children and a husband she protected and ordered about. Instead—well, Thomas said she was sleeping with men from the bar, and probably for money.
>
> But what did it matter? The two pictures of Maisie stood side by side on the empty space—and cancelled each other out. Both were true. Both were untrue. (LL, p. 158)

Reality is ugly, formless, chaotic. Society is fragmented into warring nations and idealogies. The words "black," "white," "nation," "race" cannot be destroyed either by the imposition of an old and alien order or by a vision of utopia. But they can be contained. This is the message Martha reads in the empty veld, that the sheer spaciousness of Africa can contain the disparate races and creeds of our fragmented modern world. For her the empty space of Africa comprehends contrarieties and cancels out contradictions. However "sere" the veld may be, for Martha it replaces "her old nurse, the sea," as the magna mater who soothes, sustains, and nourishes.

Martha makes an Eriksonian gesture in turning to her environment for a metaphor for her self and confirmation of her identity. But because she misconstrues what she sees, her achievement is only partial. Like her society, Martha is both formless and fragmented. Her mistake, she realizes, has been to try to order the chaos of herself with false images. But her final metaphor for herself, derived from her interpretation of the lesson of the veld, is equally false. Martha analogizes that, as the shells and surfaces of brick and concrete which the city planners impose on the veld cannot contain the vastness of Africa, so no shell can contain her. She does not live within any shell, but comprehends them all. "Who was she then, behind the banalities of the day," behind and beyond the shells of style, shape, personality, and role? "Nothing but a soft dark receptive intelligence, that was all . . . Her mind was a soft dark empty space" (FG, p. 36). Taking an image from nature, returning for nourishment to her origins, Martha triumphantly announces that "she contained the space—she was the great bell of space, and through it crawled little creatures, among them, herself" (LL, p. 160).

Identifying herself as the great bell of space, Martha finally achieves that symbiotic fusion she has always yearned for. The "soft, shell-less creature" has merged back into the womb and become "a soft dark empty space." Martha avoids constructing her own identity by incorporating the identity of space.

Thus, through a structure of interrelated images, Lessing reveals that Martha's redelineation of herself is only partially successful. But it gives Martha the confidence of a sense of identity, however mistaken she may be about the absolute accomplishment of that achievement. Armed with that confidence, she leaves Africa and enters adulthood in London. In *The Four-Gated City* Lessing explores the limits of Martha's functional identity in examining her relation to society, again through metaphor. But unlike the shell, the lighthouse, and space, the house and the tree are virtually invisible metaphors for Martha. They are Lessing's means of evaluating what Martha can only enact.

5. MARTHA IN SOCIETY: THE HOUSE

I began by examining Martha Quest as a clinician would, reading her history psychiatrically. I then suggested that one dimension of her psychological task was aesthetic, that her growth consisted not only in mastering unresolved developmental crises, but in finding an appropriate metaphor for her self. Martha cannot achieve a sense of identity until she can articulate it.

This movement toward a sense of identity is, in fact, a spiral, moving outward in increasingly wider arcs as it pushes forward. The psychological roots of Martha's character are embedded in the most intimate and nuclear relationship in life, the primary communication between mother and child. The insufficiencies of this period of her life hinder Martha from forming mature relationships and establishing adult imtimacies. She grows insofar as she differentiates herself from this primary symbiosis; as she learns who she is, she becomes able to relate meaningfully to others.

The images by which Martha represents her self to herself succeed one another in a parallel fashion. Initially choosing private, defensive imagery—the shell, the lighthouse—she draws more boldly as she sees more widely. Looking beyond herself, she sees the world she lives in and finds there forms to express her self. Her growth toward maturity is not an inward pilgrimage but an outward quest. But as we have seen, her progress is illusory, to the extent that her most outward gesture, her image of herself as the great bell of space, permits her to reenact her infantile gesture toward fusion.

With the image of the house, as it occurs in all five volumes of *Children of Violence* but more especially in *Landlocked* and *The Four-Gated City*, Lessing illuminates these aspects of Martha's growth. Martha herself is only partly aware of the house as a metaphor. She understands it as a model of society, whose interior somehow corresponds to her psychic configurations, and she moves easily in and through it. But Lessing makes the image of the house function at a level beyond Martha's awareness, to describe both the achievement of Martha's adulthood and the limitations of that achievement. Relating the inner space of the house to the vast space of Martha's veld, Lessing indicates how Martha, who may be incapable of full maturity, can nonetheless function as an adult by using her pathology creatively.

Entering Mark Coldridge's Bloomsbury house, Martha feels "claimed" by it (FG, p. 85). In fact, by moving into that house, she is claiming herself. In part this means accepting her function in society, which she sees in terms of her housekeeping role. But more fundamentally, she lays claim to her integrated self as she allows herself to be claimed by the house, thus accepting both her body and her inner psychic organization.

For Gaston Bachelard, the shell is a "primal image" of shelter.[1] Our most primitive reaction to the other is fear, to which we react by fight or flight. The shell is both weapon and refuge, but in either case it is a defensive structure. Returning to her parents' farm from the town where she works as a secretary, Martha feels "lost and afraid . . . vividly conscious of the night outside, the vast teeming night, which was so strong, and seemed to be beating down into the room, through the low shelter of the thatch, through the frail mud walls" (MQ, p. 235). Fearing the reality of Africa, the Quests and their fellow colonials build "shells for living in," houses whose style asserts European ideas of order on the brute chaos of their environment. Mrs. Quest "planned the front of the house to open over the veld 'like the prow of a ship'" (p. 14), thus imposing her sea-loving Anglicism on the harsh inland landscape. And Mrs. Talbot's townhouse bedroom, "long, low, subdued, with shell-coloured curtains . . . had a look of chaste withdrawal from the world" (PM, p. 74). Visiting her, Martha must look out of the windows "to assure herself this was in fact Africa. It might have vanished, she felt, so strong was the power of this room to destroy other realities" (p. 73).

Martha, whose adolescent body is as formless as Africa, has felt the aggressive power of the shells her mother imposes on her in the form of schoolgirl dresses and genteel expectations. She recognizes and is baffled by Mrs. Talbot's strength, expressed in a room "which had such a gleaming softness that it was strange it should oppose [Martha's] flesh with the hardness of real wood" (p. 75). So it is not surprising that her first response to the world she lives in should be to construct "intellectual's bastions of defence. . . . as if she, Martha, were a variety of soft, shell-less creature whose survival lay in the strength of those walls. Reaching out in all directions from behind it, she clutched at the bricks of arguments, the stones of words, discarding any that might not fit into the building" (p. 94).

But Martha learns that the shell is a frail bastion. Her parents' house "had sunk to its knees under the blows of the first wet season after the Quests had left it, as if the shambling structure had been held upright only by the spirit of the family in it" (LL, p. 190). And Mark's house, for him though not for Martha a shell, is a façade of gentility, "in a dreadful state beneath its surface of order" (FG, p. 111), as Martha discovers shortly after she moves in. The shell repudiates its environment, opposes it, as the Quests and Mrs. Talbot and Mark assert their values and ideas of order on an alien world. But that world is strong enough to crush any shell; on the veld "bushes and trees, held at bay so long (but only just, only very precariously) by the Quests' tenancy, came striding in, marching over the fragments of substance[2] originally snatched from the bush, to destroy the small shelter for the English family that they had built between teeming earth and brazen African sky" (LL, p. 15). And when Ottery Bartlett visits Mark's house, bringing the ugly reality of espionage in lieu of a gift, not all the oriental rugs and cut-glass sherry glasses in Bloomsbury can prevent Mark's nervous breakdown (FG, p. 173).

More importantly, the shell is a primitive and unsatisfactory abode because it impedes the movement of its inhabitant. Clearly, for certain creatures, shells are the ideal habitation. For creatures who exude their shells, their house fits their bodies, is uniquely theirs. But the creatures who live in shells in *Children of Violence* are hermit crabs, appropriating cast-off shelters and conforming (by contortion, if necessary) to their contours.

As long as Martha lives in a "shallow town house of thin brick, and cement and tin" (LL, p. 15), she perpetuates the mind/body split which marks her imperfect achievement of a sense of identity. Retreating into that shell, Martha turns her back on the source of her identity, the open space of the African veld. And by living horizontally, in a one-story space, she is ignoring the complexities of her psyche. She acknowledges the dimensions of her self when she moves into a house that "was tall rather than wide, reached up, stretched down, was built layer on layer, but shadowy above and below the shallow mid-area" (p. 15). In that house is represented her bodiliness, her fragmented psyche, and her unique mode of relating those fragments. Paradoxically, it is in that London town house that Martha utilizes the lesson of the African veld. Enclosed and domesticated, space is no longer a threat to Martha's growth, but an arena for it.

Erikson describes a woman's body as "the morphological model of care" (*Insight and Responsibility*, p. 132) with an "inner space" (*Identity*, p. 266) biologically committed to bearing children. As a comprehensive theory of femininity, his formulations about inner space are questionable, founded on data assembled long ago and for other research aims. But it provides a peculiarly appropriate analysis of one aspect of Martha's problem, which includes her inability to accept her bodiliness. In the shell of her modern apartment, Martha repudiates her inner space in rejecting her motherhood. She sets Caroline free in order to free herself. Her declaration of independence is a diet that transforms the soft curves of recent maternity into a brittle shell of stylish androgeny.

In Mark's house, Martha inhabits the mid-area, caring for the children of mothers who have retreated to the shadowy bedrooms above or the murky basement below. Functioning as a woman, Martha accepts her inner space and warms the inner space of the house she lives in. Before she sees the house, she dreams of it, "a large layered house . . . full of children, not children, half-grown people, and their faces as they turned them towards her were tortured and hurt, and she saw herself, a middle-aged woman, thickened and slowed, with the face of a middle-aged woman" (FG, pp. 59–60). "It was a sad, sad dream. But not a nightmare: no fear came with it, Martha was in the dream, she was responsible for the children. She was worried, anxious: but she held the fort, she manned defenses" (p. 71).

It is one thing to retreat behind bastions of defense and another to hold the fort from within. But both fight and flight are defensive responses, and the echo of that early image of defense in Martha's dream illuminates a particular aspect of her development. She grows not by outgrowing her handicaps, but by refashioning them.

The advanced definitions of motherhood and freedom by which Martha justifies her rejection of Caroline are the intellectual's bastions of defense behind which she retreats from her own powerful regressive tendencies. For her, biological maturity, the ability to bear children, activates all the unresolved conflicts of her own deprived infancy. To bear a child is to "lapse into" motherhood as into the sea, to regress to symbiotic union with a mother she never genuinely experienced. To the extent that motherhood stimulates her "regressive need for being dependent" (*Childhood and Society*, p. 92), she is wise to reject it. Part of knowing who one is consists of knowing what one dare not do.

But no traveler would get anywhere if he listened to the advice of the canny Vermont farmer, "Well, now, if I wanted to go where you want to go, I wouldn't start from here" (*Identity*, p. 265). Martha can stay where she is, huddled behind the "thin brick" walls of her "shallow town house," and let her daughter be raised by others. She can avoid coming to terms with herself by denying one aspect of herself. She can defend herself by fleeing from her problem.

Or, starting from where she is, accepting her handicap, she can move into Mark's layered house and hold the fort from there against her temptation to regress. Accepting her womanhood, even yielding to her maternal urges, she discovers that she can turn her fundamental need for being dependent into "a progressive turn toward a generative concern for dependents" (*Childhood and Society*, p. 92). She can fight her problem, and this is a measure of her mastery of it.

In Mark's kitchen Martha's orality is transformed into cooking. She has no leisure to gorge on chocolate; she has become " a conduit through which vast quantities of food from the markets of London reached the family table" (FG, p. 427). She cannot afford the luxury of nostalgia because the children need her. By acknowledging the "biological rock-bottom" (*Identity*, p. 281) of her inner space, she finds the fulfillment of a functional identity. The "basic modalities" of her activity in Mark's house reflect "the ground plan of her body" (*Identity*, p. 285).

The house is for Martha what Paul Ricoeur calls a "dialectic symbol."[3] It calls up some of her most "archaic" and regressive desires and refashions them into a model for action. Such symbols, for Ricoeur, are educative:

> The term "education" designates the movement by which man is led out of his childhood; this movement is, in the proper sense, an "erudition" whereby man is lifted out of his archaic past; but is also a *Bildung*, in the two-fold sense of an edification and an emergence of the *Bilder* or "images of man" which mark off the development of self-consciousness and open man to what they disclose. And this education, this erudition, this Bildung function as a second nature, for they remodel man's first nature. (p. 112)

When Martha feels "claimed" by her first sight of Mark's house, she is responding to its strong, traditional identity. She surrenders to one of her most infantile desires in taking the job Mark offers, in merging into the Radlett Street household where "if she chose to stay, there would be no doubt at all of how she ought to behave, to dress." But living in that house, Martha "remodels" her nature, to use Ricoeur's word—or, in Erikson's, she "redelineates" herself and "thus rebuild[s] the foundation of [her] identity" (*Identity*, p. 213). Emerging from the protective shells of adolescent pseudo-identities, entering and vivifying the tall house on Radlett Street, Martha refashions her dependency into care for dependents; as its housekeeper, she demonstrates her mature capability.

Lessing uses the image of the house to delineate Martha's peculiar psychic configuration. Martha herself is only partly aware of this aspect of the metaphor. For her, the house represents her functional identity, her activity in society. Her image of this relationship is Martha-as-housekeeper, a role in which she applies the knowledge she has acquired of her own psychic make-up to meaningful activity in the world around her. By espousing the inner space of Mark's house, she confirms her knowledge that she is a mass of disparate fragments that circulate freely through "the great bell of space"; by living there she redefines her social role.

In *Landlocked* Martha has a series of dreams in which she sees herself as a house with many rooms, filled with people who cannot communicate because they do not speak the same language (pp. 14–15, 30, 98). Baffled and frightened by her sense of inner division, she longs for something to unify her fragmented self. Retaining her architectural metaphor, she thinks a roof will give order to the house:

If she lived, precariously, in a house with half a dozen rooms, each room full of people (they being unable to leave the rooms they were in to visit the others, unable even to understand them, since they did not know the languages spoken in the other rooms) then what was she waiting for, in waiting for (as she knew she did) a man? Why, someone who would unify her elements, a man would be like a roof. (LL, p. 30)

"Quand les cimes de notre ciel se rejoindront," the poet says, "Ma maison aura un toit." When the peaks of our sky come together / My house will have a roof (Bachelard, p. 38).

In her affair with Thomas Stern, Martha thinks she has found a roof. Or, if not a roof, a loft, a room atop the others which orders the whole:

She had complained that her life had consisted of a dozen rooms, each self-contained, that she was wearing into a frazzle of shrill nerves in the effort of carrying herself, each time a whole, from one "room" to the other. But adding a new room to her house had ended the division. (LL, p. 98)

A master builder knows that "the reality of a building" does not consist in its roof.[4] Martha's affair with Thomas does not solve her problem, conceived architecturally or psychologically. In seeing the roof as an ordering element, she mistakenly sees it as the "centre" of her house (p. 98). But her experiences in the loft express only part of her identity, and she learns that it is "too high, too fragile, too small" to contain her (LL, p. 153).

Paraphrasing Lao-tse, Frank Lloyd Wright announced that "the reality of the vessel is the void within it" (Blake, pp. 332–333). He conceived of a house as "space-in-motion" in which "the contained space is allowed to move about, from room to room . . . rather than remain stagnant, boxed up in a series of interior cubicles" (Blake, p. 305). This is the fundamental principle of Wright's "organic architecture," a principle borrowed from nature and admitting nature into the interior of the house. Martha feels that "inside her [a lit space] opened up . . . because of the half dozen rooms she had to run around, looking after." Her previous encounter with that open space occurred on a drive across the veld. Then, puzzling over the irreconcilable fragments of her own and her friends' lives, she was strengthened and consoled by an experience of space so vast and overarching that it seemed to reconcile contrarieties, or at least to contain them. Remembering that moment, she reflects that "the tall lit space" inside her "was not an enemy, it was where, some time, the centre of the house would build itself" (LL, p. 29). Not until she leaves Africa, not until she moves into Mark's London town house, does she find an organic house. The tall house on Radlett Street expresses the shape of her self that Martha learned on the open veld. It is the mature expression, in architectural form, of that truth Martha first intuited in her moment of childish illumination, that her lodestone, her

conscience, her identity lies in "something central and fixed, but flowing
. . . a sense of movement, of separate things interacting and finally becoming one, but greater" (MQ, p. 200).

Martha's increasing skill at keeping house parallels her personal development. Her perception that society is fragmented evokes the same two responses that her similar discovery about herself called forth. On the one
hand, she laments the loss of an order which she assumes existed at some
prior time. Mark's house is "a house separated with the people who inhabited
it, into areas or climates, each with its own feel, or sense of individuality"
(FG, pp. 335–336). She feels that there is "no centre in the house, nothing
to hold it together (as there had been once when it was a real family house?)"
(p. 336). But this is frivolous nostalgia. Whatever the Victorian household
may have had in the way of inner order, that model will not serve for present
reality, where there can be "no resting on normality" because there are no
"ordinary people, families" (p. 340). Living as if the old structures were
meaningful drives Lynda mad; every attempt to be a "real" wife, mother, or
hostess sends her plummeting to the cellar.

Saner than Lynda and wiser than Mark, Martha does not attempt to impose old forms on present chaos. For one thing she has no inherited pattern
to offer. As her old friend Maisie's daughter Rita more jauntily announces,
"I'm a Zambesian, we are independent by nature" (p. 544). More importantly, she has felt the devastating effects of her mother's rage for order in
her own life and fears its corrosive power over her daughter. Like another
woman poet, Martha might well cry, "Christ! What are patterns for?"

Seeing in Mark's house an image of society at large—"this was the real
truth of what went on not only here but everywhere . . . a mass of fragments, like a smashed mirror" (p. 337)—Martha thinks that her special talent,
"feeling herself . . . to be a mass of fragments" (p. 336), lies in her ability
to keep things separate. "Her role in life . . . was to walk like a housekeeper in and out of different rooms, but the people in the rooms could not
meet each other or understand each other, and Martha must not expect them
to. She must not try and explain, or build bridges" (LL, p. 15). This is a
partial truth. The only way to act in and for this society is to recognize that
its disparities cannot be reconciled. But the sum of those parts does add up
to a whole, however unrecognizable it may be to a pre-Einsteinian mathema-
tician. Martha's innate intelligence is proved by her ability to grasp this new
concept of wholeness: "What an extraordinary household this was, after all,
this entity, containing such a variety of attitudes, positions! A whole. People
in any sort of communion, link, connection, make up a whole" (FG, p. 211).

Martha's intuition of the unity of fragmented parts revives her childhood illumination. "She was feeling that again, as she had before, in a

heightened, meaningful way, as if a different set of senses operated in her to enable her to *feel,* even if briefly, the connection between them all" (p. 211). Her earlier conception of housekeeping is a defection from that perception of reality she glimpsed in childhood. As a young woman in Zambesia, she was highly critical of her way of relating to other people:

> She was always creating situations full of discordant people. It did not flatter her that she could: on the contrary. If such tenuous ties she had with people, easy contact, surface friendship, yet had the strength to bring them together, what did that fact say about them, about her. . . . And it was no quality to be admired in herself that made her a focus. She was, at this time, available. (LL, p. 44)

Her self criticism devalues her real worth. The house that comprises her society is organized around a fluid, open space at its core; Martha the housekeeper is "a deputy in the centre of a house, the person who runs things, keeps things going, conducts a holding operation" (FG, p. 336). It is Martha who circulates through the house, climbing the stairs to Paul's eyrie, descending to Lynda's basement, cooking meals and drinking brandy, with Mark in the middle. "She was the great bell of space, and through it crawled little creatures, among them, herself." Transposed from the veld to London, the great bell becomes what Bachelard calls "felicitous space" (p. xxxi).

Within this permissive space, a new society comes into being. None of the young people—Francis, Paul, Jill, Gwen—has "any intention of behaving as . . . previous generations behaved." Instead they undertake what Martha identifies as "that process of *being stripped,*[5] being sharpened and sensitized, which uses the forms of ordinary life merely as tools, methods" (FG, p. 428). For them "the stripping process begins so young it is as if an announcement has been made: Don't trouble with anything else; this is what you have to do" (p. 429). For the older people in the house, divestiture is difficult. Mark is "stripped" (p. 282) by the trauma of Colin's defection to Russia and the subsequent nastiness that enters his comfortable drawing room, but his basic orientation is toward the past. After the cataclysm, exiled to the radiation-free deserts of North Africa, he broods over the lost order; "the word England, England, makes me ache, makes me stretch out my arms . . . all those sweet fields and good people gone" (p. 610).

What the young people acknowledge is their soft shell-less vulnerability, and within the protected space of the house they dare to. There they create a new order, as organic as Wright's houses, exuding a shell that precisely fits their bumpy contours. As in Martha's dream city, inside the house there is "harmony, order—joy" (p. 134).

What constitutes this order, this harmony, is difficult to analyze because its essence is its imprecision. In Mark's house it is the circulating space that unites fragments without attempting to fuse them. In Francis's commune, later, there is no formal structure. The community is a loose confederation of "those who were 'eccentric' or slightly ill," drop-outs from Henry Matheson's world of slots and definitions, "unwilling or unable to live according to the norms of the time" (p. 564). Nothing about the community is regimented or even "formulated." "Yet a feeling of community remained even when we lived apart," Francis recalls (p. 565).

But the house and the commune exist in the context of a larger society, which is inimical to them. Around the city of Martha's dreams "rose the encircling shadow city of people who looked enviously in at the privileged one" (p. 134). The shadow city is the established order, with a power structure we have come to accept as inevitable: rulers, soldiers, brokers, merchants, above all words. What the Establishment demands is clarity; what it cannot tolerate is imprecision. The rulers of the outer city ask for the secret of the inner city's harmony and when the reply comes back "that the secret could not be sold, or taken: it could only be earned, or accepted as a gift" (p. 135), they are enraged and sack the city. When Francis and his friends are asked to discuss their community on television, they are not prepared for the audience's response. They had not foreseen that "no one was able to believe in the possibility of something unorganised, unregimented, undoctrinaire" (p. 570).

The Establishment is the arm of the old order. In one setting it manifests its power as an imposition on nature. In Africa colonizers build their English bungalows on the veld, unable to comprehend and therefore terrified of vast, teeming space. Baffled by the disparities of race and clan and subculture, they regiment Africa with passes and color bars and an elaborate policy of Apartheid. The Establishment is motivated by fear, but the shell of order it creates for its protection becomes a formidable weapon.

"Suppose Lynda had been a fifteen-year-old in a society where 'hearing voices' was not sick, but a capacity some people had?" wonders Martha. Suppose, that is, that Lynda had grown up in felicitous space, as the children in Mark's house do? "But she had had no such luck; had been made a psychological cripple before she was twenty" (p. 496). With that example of society's malevolence before her, Martha works to maintain the sanctuary that is Mark's house, to preserve a space in which the new society can come into being.

But by the same token that the Establishment is powerful enough to impose its alien patterns on the formless fecundity of Africa, it is strong enough to bring Martha's house down, with an order from the London County Council. The Radlett Street house is "to be compulsorily purchased for demolition, or redevelopment" (p. 499). It wrecks Francis' commune with an "order for dispersal" signed by his politician Aunt, Phoebe (p. 593).

And finally it blows itself up, in order to begin again as "Newest England" in some uncontaminated, colonized space (p. 581). In Mark's house on Radlett Street, Martha has found a hospital to heal her psychic wounds. Its many rooms house the fragments of her self, as the central core of circulating space unites them. It is a structural expression of the identity she has slowly accrued, and a model of society which both corroborates that identity and gives it scope for meaningful action. But her refuge and her arena are taken from her. She must leave Mark's house to the County Council and "step into the dark" (p. 555).

It is equally important to note that although Martha is forced to leave Mark's house, she does not do so reluctantly. There is a note of emancipation in her reflection that, "Oh yes, she really was on her way out and away. No longer was this house her responsibility" (p. 556).

For Bachelard the house is one of man's fundamental images of felicitous space because it corresponds to his dual consciousnesses of centrality and verticality (Bachelard, p. 17). In *Landlocked* and *The Four-Gated City* Lessing uses the image of the many-storyed house to explore the conflict in Martha between these two consciousnesses. We have seen how, by living in the "shallow mid-area" of Mark's house, Martha has acknowledged and come to terms with the central fact of her womanhood. What she cannot come to terms with is the restriction of her activity—and her identity—to the inner space of Mark's house. For there are no attics in that house, and the basement is available to Martha only on Lynda's terms.

Erikson defines ego-identity as a "sense of the reality of the Self within social reality . . . the ego's synthesizing power in the light of its central psychosocial function" (*Identity*, p. 211). Martha's role as housekeeper represents her achievement of ego-identity, a remarkable accomplishment in the light of the personal and social handicaps she has had to surmount. But she is not satisfied with her accomplishment. She constantly opposes to the idea of ego-identity her own notion of the Self, which she searches for by moving down into madness or up into expanded consciousness.

Mark's house is felt not only as a refuge but as a menace to Martha. When she enters it for the first time, she feels not only claimed but "attacked" by it (FG, p. 85). She takes the job Mark offers and assumes responsibility for the house in part because she can no longer "tolerate" the anonymity of the streets, her aimless "walking and riding and talking the time away under this name or that . . . until one felt like an empty space without boundaries" (p. 17). But with at least part of herself she knows that this undefined aimlessness is "the best thing she had known" (p. 35). The house offers her a name, a functional identity—"She was very definitely Martha"—but it limits her exploration of her Self; "The dullness, the inertia, of being at home took over. And very far was she from the open-pored receptive being who hadn't a name" (p. 47).

Martha is ambivalent toward Mark's house. She associates the high empty space of self-contemplation with Jack, who "could not go on as he was now, he'd fall. And so would she if she did not move out of this high stretch of herself" (p. 38). The house that Jack builds is, unlike Mark's, "a fantasy house" (p. 382), but Martha is drawn to it because in Jack's attic, as in Thomas Stern's loft, she is almost out of the house, separated from empty space only by the roof.

As we have seen, Martha's identification of herself with open space is a reformulation of her most regressive gesture. To seek herself by losing her self in sexual transport is peculiarly appealing, and particularly dangerous to her. Thomas and Jack and their attics are bad for her. She is drawn to Jack because, like Thomas', his "flesh breathed time and death; but his mind and his memory moved along another line parallel to it" (p. 50). He is a divided self, in other words, and his insatiable hunger and fondness for cocoa echo Martha's orality. Every time she goes to Jack's attic, Martha is revisiting her younger self and reinforcing her pathology.

Despite her attraction to Jack's attic, Martha returns to Mark's house as long as it's there because she has "debts to pay" (p. 38). She thinks of Caroline, "the two men she had married so absurdly," her mother, but what she must in fact pay is a debt to herself. She must make reparation not to anyone else, but to herself for her impoverished womanhood. Caring for Francis and Paul does nothing for Caroline, but it restores to Martha her own maternal inner space. Her "marriage" to Mark is, if anything, even more "absurd" than her previous marriages to Douglas Knowell and Anton Hesse, but it is an attempt to redefine intimacy which teaches Martha finally that she is "unmarriageable" (p. 285). And in Mark's house at last, Martha comes to terms with her relationship to her mother, accepts pain, acknowledges her deprivation, and works herself free of the bondage of the past.

To develop herself, Martha needs the house. "One could not move on before all the debts were paid" (p. 38). But as long as she lives in the house, she believes she can do no more than revise the past. "You start growing on your own account," she maintains, "when you've worked through what you're landed with. Until then, you're paying off debts" (p. 432). In the social nexus of the house, she pays her debts, thinking all the while that she is thus postponing the lonely, dangerous exploration of space that may lead her to her self.

Like Bluebeard's castle, Mark's house has locked doors that tempt Martha. There are areas that must be out of bounds as long as she has responsibilities to the others who live in the house, "responsibility, that is, to the normal, the usual" (p. 38). Lynda's basement is out of bounds, so long as Martha has duties on the floors above it. That cellar is "a place to get out of as fast as possible" if you want to preserve your sanity; or if you want instead to explore the parameters of your self, it is "a place to study, to make sense of, to sink oneself into" (p. 462). So Martha feels it, and is tempted by it, but is prevented from exploring its dimensions not only by Mark but by Lynda, who needs Martha to be her custodian: "Don't Martha, don't, don't, don't, Martha," she whimpers as Martha yields to the lure of cellar insanity. " 'You mustn't get locked up, Martha. I can't do it, but you can.' . . . This message was perfectly intelligible to Martha. She nodded. Of course: Those who could had a responsibility for those who could not. . . . But—first things first. Now she must be normal, because Lynda must not be upset by her losing control" (p. 492).

As long as Martha inhabits and orders Mark's house, she must postpone the lonely contemplation of her various selves she believes may teach her who she truly is. Emerging from Lynda's cellar, "she was curious, and angry with herself that she had not done this before—good God, this door (like so many others, she must suppose) had been standing here, ready for her to walk in any time she wished" (p. 468).

"The fundamental human significance of architecture stems from this," says Laing, that "the physical environment unremittingly offers us possibilities of experience, or curtails them" (*Politics of Experience*, p. 33). Both Martha and Lessing would agree, but they would differ in their identification of the most facilitating environment for Martha. When she is temporarily freed from her duties in Mark's house, Martha goes gladly to "the top of the house" (p. 502) that Paul owns, so that she can have, as she puts it, "privacy to explore my own being" (p. 501). She invites and experiences a prolonged psychotic episode in which she nearly succeeds in losing herself forever. What saves her is the call to return to Mark's house and resume her duties. As she shakily leaves the top floor of Paul's house, she "thought that the last few weeks had taken her right over the edge into a permanent stage of being plugged into the sea of sound; and that its main, persistent, hammering, never-sleeping voice was the Devil's, the voice of the self-punisher" (p. 523). But after a few weeks back home at Radlett Street, "she noted that because she was very busy, very worried over Lynda, her own Devil retreated" (p. 527).

So long as Martha remains in Mark's house, she can maintain a sense of ego-identity. In that house she can restrain her regressive impulses by transforming them into creative activity. But by constructing a house without an attic and with only limited access to the cellar, Lessing has defined the limits of Martha's psychological maturity. Martha has not achieved a fully

Eriksonian sense of identity because the society which confirms her and in which she functions is a *temenos,* a protected space within society at large, where Martha can safely operate.

By opening all the doors of her house metaphor, Lessing has both asserted the Eriksonian definition of identity as a relationship between self and society and announced the particular limitations of her protagonist. But just as Mark's house is too frail to withstand the assaults of the hostile world outside its walls, so Lessing's metaphor is inadequate to define her protagonist's relation to that world. To make that statement, Lessing employs another pattern of images, clustering around the controlling metaphor of the tree.

6. THE END OF THE QUEST: THE TREE

An examination of the permutations of the image of the tree in *Children of Violence* reveals its multifoliate usefulness. On one level it describes Martha's development toward identity. On another, it comments on the relationship between Martha and society. It is a metaphor of growth but also of relatedness. With it Lessing attempts to resolve a problem that has both psychological and literary implications.

As a metaphor of growth, the image of the tree is directly related to that of the house. It both defines and confirms the account Lessing has given of Martha's idiosyncratic development. Many readers see *Children of Violence*, and *The Four-Gated City* in particular, as an assertion of the essential privacy of self-discovery. Martha's "inner life," according to one critic, is "a life of obsessive self-concentration which denies the real significance of others and makes it clear that, in her case at least, the good woman's actions, however socially useful, do not reflect her essence."[1] I think, on the contrary, that Lessing's use of the tree image in *Children of Violence* makes it clear that she, like Erikson, believes that a sense of identity is necessarily rooted in a relationship with others, that identity is the result of a healthy symbiosis between self and society.

As a metaphor of epigenetic growth, the tree image further allies Lessing with Erikson. Martha does not, it becomes clear, break with her past in breaking through to a new level of consciousness. Her excursions into madness and her development of extrasensory perception are, rather, extensions of her ordinary capacities made necessary by the conditions of the world she lives in. Her growth is evolutionary, not revolutionary—organic, natural, like a tree's.

The questions of identity and of the relationship between the self and society have literary as well as psychological ramifications. A *bildungsroman* can be described in terms of the process it records or in terms of its resolution. As a process of growth toward identity, all *bildungsromane* are structured as a dialectic between "a set of influences from outside" and the "formative dynamism within the organism" (Pascal, p. 24) which reacts with them to create the protagonist's sense of himself. Some *bildungsromane* resolve this dialectic by asserting its continuation; self and society are and always will be antithetical. The discovery of the self is equated with the discovery of one's necessary alienation. In others, the tensions between the individual and society are resolved by a movement "out of inwardness into social activity, out of subjectivity into objectivity" (Pascal, p. 299). With the image of the tree, Lessing makes a generic assertion, aligning *Children of Violence* with *Wilhelm Meister* as that kind of *bildungsroman* which records a synthetic resolution to the dialectic of growth. For a tree has roots and gives shade, depends on its environment and contributes to it. The tree is an ecological image.

As a generic metaphor the tree is less satisfying than as a metaphor of growth. As the latter it is consistent with what Lessing has revealed about Martha's peculiar limitations, as well as her unique talents. But the image of the tree makes its generic statement by a willful superimposition of meaning which turns Martha from the particular into the exemplary "individual conscience in its relations with the collective."[2] While Lessing's use of the metaphor makes it clear that she does not intend her protagonist's achievement of identity to be an exercise in solipsism,[3] it does not succeed in defining precisely the manner of Martha's final relation to society. For the identity of society, no less than of the protagonist, is at issue.

Distinguishing the various uses to which Lessing puts the image of the tree, it thus becomes possible not only to separate psychological from literary questions, but to isolate the particular weakness of *Children of Violence* as a *bildungsroman*.

I. The Tree as a Metaphor of Growth

Martha's capacity for growth is, as we have seen, indicated by her innovativeness. Unlike her parents, who live by outmoded fictions, Martha continually refashions her images of herself and of the world she lives in. In this she surpasses even her mentors, of whom the most significant is Thomas Stern.

One of the important stages in Martha's growth to identity is her affair with Thomas, with whom she is "driven . . . back and back into regions of herself she had not known existed" (LL, p. 101). Sex, for Martha and Thomas, is an experience of transcending the boundaries of individuality to be in touch with "enormous forces" (p. 153) they do not understand. But although Martha does not understand until later, with Jack, what those forces are, she does know that she has been irrevocably changed by her experience with Thomas: "Some force, some power, had taken hold of them both, and had made such changes in her—what, soul? (but she did not even know what words she must use) psyche? being?—that now she was changed and did not understand herself" (p. 218).

Thomas also senses the extraordinary nature of their relationship and speculates that he and Martha are "something new" (p. 116). He introduces Martha to the idea of mutation which underlies the latter part of her quest for identity, the idea that the individual's response to new social configurations must be not the repetition of old forms, but the creation of new ones.

Thomas associates mutation not with growth, however, but with insanity. "Perhaps there'll be a mutation," he muses to Martha, "Perhaps that's why we are all so sick. Something new is trying to get born through our thick skins. I tell you, Martha, if I see a sane person, then I know he's mad. You know, the householders. It's we who are nearest to being—what's needed" (p. 116).

Thomas is sick because "the elm tree and safety's finished" (p. 168). "It was once like this," he tells Martha:

> A child was born in a house that had a tree outside it. It was an elm tree. His grandfather had planted it. The child grew up while the tree shed its leaves and grew them again. He quarrelled with his father, but afterwards lay under the elm tree and felt at peace. He slept with his first girl under the elm tree, and their baby was put to sleep under the elm tree, and when his wife died she was buried under the elm tree, and as an old man, he stood at his gate and looked at the tree and thought: That tree has been with me all my life. (LL, p. 117)

But the Nazis have invaded Poland and cut down the elm trees. Thomas is no longer a peasant from Sochaczen, but the wandering Jew. Colin Coldridge is the norm now, Colin who "had always been a scientist" (FG, p. 315), is equally a citizen of the Soviet Union and of England. He is the man without a country, who lives not under an elm tree but under an Einsteinian star, and, as Thomas says:

> That star's got a different time scale from us. We are born under that star and make love under it and put our children to sleep under it and are buried under it. The elm tree is out of date, it's had its day. Now we try all the time, day and night to understand: that star has a different time scale, we are like midges compared to the star. And that's why you're all on edge and why I'm sick although I'm a peasant from Sochaczen. (LL, p. 117)

Although Thomas knows that the world has changed, he is incapable of changing with it. The force that "took hold of them both" in sex has "changed" Martha, but not Thomas, who simply cannot "understand." His suggestion that he and Martha are "what's needed" in a world without elm trees is predicated on his bitter conviction that they are both sick. It is not an optimistic response to reality, but a despairing gesture of nihilism. Thomas cannot survive his vision and goes mad. Later Martha has a dream (pp. 201–203) in which Thomas, who could envisage only one tree, the elm, is hanged on another, the gallows. He cannot adapt, so he is destroyed.

In his book *The Master Builders*, Peter Blake observes that Frank Lloyd

Wright had "two major difficulties of a philosophical sort in designing a sky-scraper: first, as a believer in an architecture close to nature, he had a hard time justifying a tall, upright, seemingly antinature building; and, second, his obsession with the twin concepts of continuity and plasticity . . . made it difficult to approach the design of a tall, multicellular building." Wright re-solved this dilemma "by going to the one source in nature which did indeed suggest a way of building a tall structure: the form of a tree" (p. 347). Mar-tha's growth to identity is possible, at least in part, because like Wright and unlike Thomas, she is able to translate the essential shape of natural struc-tures into contemporary, urban forms. She is able to adapt, and thus able to grow.

Her initial response to London echoes Thomas's despair; there are "no trees in this street," she laments, "not one tree: therefore, no roots" (FG, p. 8). Gradually she comes to see that this rootless city has the same spatial configurations as the African veld, in which her identity is rooted. When she sees herself as "a tiny coloured blob, among other blobs, on top of a bus, or in a street" (p. 16), she evokes the memory of herself and Jack Dobie as "two tiny ant-like figures" (LL, p. 160) driving across the empty space of the veld. Increasingly she portrays the city with images drawn from nature: "the street surfaces were never level; they were always 'up,' being altered, dug into, pitted, while men rooted in them to find tangled pipes in wet earth . . . buildings momentarily form, change colour like vegetation, dissolve, re-form" (FG, p. 288). Thus she makes it possible for herself to draw suste-nance from London, just as she was initially nourished by the soil of her native Africa.

Martha is like Frank Lloyd Wright in her initial response to the modern urban landscape. She sees it as unnatural: "If one were to wade through earth in Africa, around one's legs roots: tree roots, thick, buried branches . . . But walking here, it would be through heavy unaired rootless soil, where electricity and telephone and gas tubes ran and knotted and twined" (p. 8). City dwellers' houses are "shells and surfaces of brick and concrete" (MQ, p. 230) which separate man from nature, just as the shell of Martha's appearance interposes a defensive barrier between her true inner self and the alien world she must perforce inhabit. The shell house bears no relation to its environment, just as Matty the shell does not reflect the true shape of the essential Martha.

But in Mark's house, Martha resolves these antagonisms between nature and civilization, between self and social function. She first encounters the space that provides her with a metaphor for her self on the veld, but she re-discovers it in Mark's house, which, like a tree, is "a delicate balance of forces, each restraining the other through an infinite number of strands and fibers which make the tree a continuous organism" (Blake, p. 348). In her role as keeper of that house, she also discovers that not only does she inhabit organic space, she is herself the great bell of space, which contains and comprehends contradictions and chaos. In that tall house Martha obeys the poet's injunction:

> If you want to achieve the existence of a tree,
> Invest it with inner space, this space
> That has its being in you.
> (Rilke, quoted in Bachelard, p. 200)

Martha achieves the existence of a tree by identifying herself with the tree outside her window in Mark's house. The young Martha, who creeps from shell to shell, sees the tree as a shelter and herself as a bird. "She was like a bird flitting from branch to darkening branch of an immense tree. . . . She read like a bird collecting twigs for a nest" (MQ, p. 200). Having passed through the initiatory stages on her road to self-discovery, Martha dares as Mark's housekeeper to assume the proud posture of the tree itself, the "form that eliminates / Hazards of wind" because of its rootedness (Rilke, quoted in Bachelard, p. 240). But her mother's announcement that she is coming to London recalls her past vulnerability to Martha, and she struggles to establish her independent selfhood so that she can withstand remembered pain. Day after day she sits in her room, staring out the window, asking:

> *Who* watched? She sat in the chair. Outside the elegant tall window with its graceful frame and panes, a tree. Nothing was more extraordinary and marvellous than that tree, a being waving its green limbs from a grey surface. Beneath the surface was a structure of roots whose shape had a correspondence with the shape and spread of its branches. This curious being that stood opposite the window was a kind of conduit for the underground rivers of London, which rushed up its trunk, diffusing outwards through a hundred branches to disperse into the air and stream upwards, to join the damp cloud cover of the London sky. She felt she had never seen a tree before. The word "tree" was alien to the being on the pavement. Tree, tree, she kept saying, as she said Martha, Martha, feeling the irrelevance of these syllables, which usurped the reality of the living structure. (FG, p. 215)

On one side of the window is a curious being named tree, on the other one named Martha. Both are conduits, one of water, the other of food (Martha has identified herself as a conduit of food from the markets of London to the family table in Mark's kitchen). And the word "Martha" is as alien to the being in the room as the word "tree" is to the being on the pavement. Both are living structures whose realities are belied and betrayed by any labels.

By further contemplating the tree, Martha learns what that reality is, although it eludes articulation:

> She could sit on a chair, or rather feel herself held on soft support, and look at a

tree, or rather a brownish-grey thing that stuck out of the pavement and became a green mass, which was made up of a thousand little pieces of green—look, feel, as empty as a pool. Who? Into the pool came a word, sycamore. . . . She saw it; into it she fitted herself, saw the world on either side of her head in two outstretching expanses of grass, bushes. Who are you then? Why, me, of course, who else, horse, woman, man, or tree, a glittering faceted individuality of breathing green, here is the sense of me, nameless, recognizable only to me. (p. 221)

With that confidence, she can face not only her mother but her future, as she goes on to discover the full dimensions of her self.

Martha begins to be conscious of the process of growth, to theorize about it, in *The Four-Gated City*, when she compares it to a tree:

In every life there is a curve of growth, or a falling away from it; there is a central pressure, like sap forcing up a trunk, along a branch, into last year's wood, and there, from a deadlooking eye, or knot, it bursts again in a new branch, in a shape that is inevitable but known only to itself until it becomes visible. (p. 192)

This theory of growth contains two elements. First, it avers that one becomes what one is inevitably meant to be. Over and over, Martha reiterates her conviction that in growing to identity, one realizes what was latent in one's beginnings. To Jack's other girl friend, Joanna, she says "I remember finding out some time before—that that is what learning is. You suddenly understand something you've understood all your life" (p. 97). She thinks of her therapy with Dr. Lamb as an experience of growth in which "one talked, one did this or that: finally, one 'heard' for the first time what one's life had been saying over and over again, in various ways, for years" (p. 225). Even in the table-rapping world of Rosa Mellendip, Martha can discern the "rule, or law . . . the paradox that one could never be told what one did not already know, though of course the 'knowing' might be hidden from oneself" (p. 353).

But this preordained shape of one's identity will be a "new branch"; the self one discovers may bear no relation to anything one has known about oneself before. Lessing's epigraph to Part One of *Landlocked*, her first use of Sufi teachings in *Children of Violence*, is a parable about identity:

The Mulla walked into a shop one day.
The owner came forward to serve him.
'First things first,' said Nasrudin; 'did you see me walk into your shop?'
'Of course.'
'Have you ever seen me before?'
'Never in my life.'
'Then how do you know it is me?'

How do I know I am me? I know because I can be nothing but what I was meant to be; the self I discover will be consistent with my earliest intimations of it. Throughout her history, Martha returns to the memory of her moment of illumination as a child on the veld, her insight into the nature of the universe and her place in it. This is her lodestone, the measure by which she evaluates succeeding experiences. It provides her with a sense of "what was real in her" (LL, p. 13), which leads her to reject certain possibilities as wrong—she knows, for instance, that to stay on indefinitely in Zambesia as Mr. Robinson's top secretary "would be one of the bad, serious decisions of her life" (LL, p. 8).

But in order to discover the shape of one's self that has been preordained to emerge, one may need to develop new senses. Martha tells Joanna that learning is finding out what you've known all along, "but in a new way" (FG, p. 97). With Dr. Lamb she hears what her life had been saying for years because "Dr. Lamb . . . embodied that growing principle in life which fed one, developed one, so that one had 'ears' where one hadn't before." "Living," she muses—and she might as easily have said "growing"—is "simply a process of developing different 'ears,' senses, with which one 'heard,' experienced, what one couldn't before" (p. 225).

Lessing prefaces Book Four of *The Four-Gated City*, the section of the novel in which Martha forays into madness with Lynda and on her own and discovers her powers of extrasensory perception, with a quotation from Indries Shah:

> Sufis believe that . . . humanity is evolving towards a certain destiny. We are all taking part in that evolution. Organs come into being as a result of a need for specific organs . . . In this age of the transcending of time and space, the complex of organs is concerned with the transcending of time and space. What ordinary people regard as sporadic and occasional bursts of telepathic and prophetic power are seen by the Sufi as nothing less than the first stirrings of these same organs. (FG, p. 426)[4]

This is simply a mystical restatement of the principle of epigenesis, originally applied by Aristotle to embryology and reapplied to psychological development by Erikson, that the individual develops by producing new parts, previously nonexistent. Whether these parts be organs or senses or modes of relating to other people, the process is the same: the new evolves from the old, but responds creatively when the environment changes. As her innovativeness enables Martha to make sense of the world she lives in, so her ability to develop new ways of seeing and hearing makes it possible for her to discover and develop her self.

Martha explores her self through a variety of new senses, through sex with Thomas and Jack, the occult with Rosa Mellendip, madness and extrasensory perception with Lynda—and always dreams. She continually compares herself to a child learning to walk (pp. 176–473), thus recalling her early statement to Jack of the task we all assume with our humanity:

> A baby is born with infinite possibilities for being good. But there's no escaping it,
> it's like having to go down into a pit, a terrible dark blind pit, and then you fight
> your way up and out . . . The mistake is, to think there is a way of not having to
> fight your way out. Everyone has to. And if you don't, then it's too bad, no one's
> going to cry for you, it's no loss, only to yourself. (p. 68)

We have seen Martha work her way out of the pit of her own psychological
handicaps, and we now are invited to watch her move on, like a baby learning to walk, to discover new dimensions of her self.

Watching one's feet take one step after another is a narcissistic form of
contemplation appropriate for a baby, but self-indulgent for an adult. For
Erikson, at least, the apex of the developmental scale is not the adolescent
achievement of identity, but the mature exercise of generativity, which he
admits "is not an elegant word,"[5] but which means the assumption of responsibility for future generations. It can be argued however,[6] that *The Four-
Gated City* asserts that Martha's identity lies in her acceptance of the contin-
uing quest, that she does not achieve a fixed identity but learns "that most
important thing, which was that one simply had to go on, take one step after
another: this process in itself held the keys" (p. 556).

II. The Tree as a Generic Metaphor

Martha's use of the tree image to define the process of growth links her
with Erikson insofar as it expresses an epigenetic idea of development. But
the larger issue which makes Eriksonian psychology relevant to the study of
the *bildungsroman* is his assertion of the interrelatedness and interdepen-
dence of self and society. *Wilhelm Meister* and *The Portrait of a Lady*, for
instance, are both Eriksonian *bildungsromane*, although one has a happy
ending and the other is tragic. Both assert the necessary bonds that link the
individual to the society around him. Wilhelm confidently assumes his place
in German society at the end of the *Lehrjahre*, having learned the lesson of
the Tower, "hier oder nirgends ist Amerika." Lothario's definition of the
here-and now-ness of adventure is ironically echoed by Isabel Archer in her
sad discovery that "one must choose a corner and cultivate that." The society she returns to is what Dorothy Van Ghent has called "Osmond's claustral
house," but she chooses it in preference to the freedom Goodwood offers
her in America because "it is there . . . that she has placed roots, found a
crevice in which to grow straightly and freshly, found a fertilizing, civilizing
relationship between consciousness and circumstances."[7]

As Martha uses the tree to explain what she means by growth, so Lessing uses the tree image to announce what kind of *bildungsroman* she has
written. She uses it first to assert the Eriksonian postulate that an individual

achieves a sense of identity only within a social context. Martha, we have seen, is ambivalent about the house that provides her with that context. Her experience of the house on Radlett Street is one of enclosure, what the Germans call *hemmung*. But there are doors and windows and, on the other side of the window in her room, a tree with which she identifies in her searching encounter with her self.

Martha imagines that all routes to self-knowledge lead through doors (LL, p. 98; FG, pp. 286, 354, 356, 468, 489) and that the process of taking one step after another holds the keys to those doors (FG, pp. 354, 431). For if one takes one step after another, one will finally get to a place "where at least one could begin to see the way out, and forward" (FG, p. 472).

Beyond the door is the street that Martha discovered as "the best thing" about London when she first arrived. Anonymously roaming London's streets, Martha extends the exploration of herself and her place in the universe which began with her childhood illumination on the open veld. In comparison, only "a dull light" burns behind the windows of the houses that line the open streets (FG, p. 36).

Just so, when she was younger, did Martha distinguish between enclosure and freedom, although in Africa the terms were different:

> On and on; the town was a long way behind, the farm was not yet reached; and in between these two lodestones, this free and reckless passage through warmed blue air. How terrible that it must always be the town or the farm; how terrible this decision always one thing or the other, and the exquisite flight between them so short, so fatally limited. (MQ, p. 230).

But although Martha's longing for open space is keen, it is not unqualified. "The exquisite flight" is "reckless" as well as free, reckless with its double connotation of daring and not-caring. Later, Martha senses that Jack will "fall and break his crown" if he continues the lonely exploration of the open space of heightened consciousness which he reaches through sex. He will fall not only because he has scaled the heights, but because he has abjured responsibility: "I want you to have my baby," he tells Martha, "And I want Nancy and Joan and Melinda to have my babies. . . . But I won't be a father" (FG, p. 67). Martha responds angrily by accusing Jack of irresponsibility, of wanting to "put cuckoos in nests" (p. 66). Jack is "rootless" (p. 38), and clearly, for Martha, being rooted means more than knowing one's origins: it also means assuming one's place in an ecology, acknowledging that one is related to others in mutual responsibility. "What's the use of imagining impossibly marvellous ways of living," she asks, "they aren't anywhere near us, are they? You've got to accept" (p. 68).

Martha's longing to get out, her feeling that she is balked in her progress to self-discovery by her responsibilities in Mark's house ("she had never been less Martha than now . . . she was never alone," p. 369), is continually checked by her horror of being "rootless." If the tree with which Martha identifies in her quest for herself grows outside the house, she nonetheless must remain in it if she is to be rooted. At the end of Part Four of *The Four-Gated City*, Martha seems finally to have accepted this necessity. The final sentences of the novel assert the social nexus of the quest for identity:

> She walked, quiet, while the house began to reverberate: a band had started up. She walked beside the river while the music thudded, feeling herself as a heavy impervious insensitive lump that, like a planet doomed always to be dark on one side, had vision in front only, a myopic searchlight blind except for the tiny three-dimensional path open immediately before her eyes in which the outline of a tree, a rose, emerged, then submerged in dark. She thought, with the dove's voices of her solitude: Where? But *where*. How? Who? No, but *where*, where . . . Then silence and the birth of a repetition: *Where?* Here. Here?
>
> Here, where else, you fool, you poor fool, where else has it been, ever . . .
> (p. 559)

The relevant question is neither how nor even who, but where. Where is the context in which one discovers one's self? And the answer seems unequivocal: here.

But where is here? Martha is not inside the house at the end of the book, but alone, taking one step after another on a private path toward self-discovery, signified by "the outline of a tree." The particular society in which she has been able to sink her roots has been dispersed by the larger society in which it exists and with which it is at odds.

If *The Four-Gated City* had concluded at the end of Part Four, it would be a deeply pessimistic *bildungsroman*. It makes the emotional statement that there is and can be no mutually sustaining relationship between the individual and society because society will not tolerate innovation. Martha's attempt to create a society within Mark's house which will conform to the dimensions of her self and enhance the lives of everyone who lives there is brutally canceled by the order from the County Council for the demolition of the house. Confronted with this imperturbable and impregnable society, Martha comes to believe that "if society is so organized . . . that it will not admit what one knows to be true, will not admit it, that is, except as it comes out perverted, through madness, then it is through madness and its variants it must be sought after" (p. 357).

Martha is rescued from the consequences of this line of reasoning by the appendix to *The Four-Gated City*, in which Lessing destroys that hostile world by fiat and gives Martha a context once again. The island on which she is shipwrecked with a group of survivors from the nuclear holocaust which devastates Britain becomes the setting for a new society which, in its harmony and order, fulfills the models implicit in Mark's house and Francis' commune. Forced like a band of Crusoes to create a new civilization, Martha and her comrades engender a community which gives them hope for the future of the race.

The appendix makes *Children of Violence* a new kind of *bildungsroman* in which the protagonist neither rejects society nor is reclaimed by it, but recreates it. But we can legitimately ask whether Lessing has created a new kind of *bildungsroman* by failing to obey the rules of the genre. She can posit a Goetheian synthesis to the dialectic between the individual conscience and the collective, between self and society, only by asserting that Mark's house and Martha's island are models of society. But clearly they are alternative societies, the one at odds with the real world and the other a replacement for it. In her description of Martha's development, Lessing defines her partial and incomplete achievement of Eriksonian ego-identity with reference to the partiality of Mark's house. Martha is portrayed as achieving a limited maturity, a sense of identity which is functional only in a protected context. Mark's house is the closest approximation to reality Martha can tolerate, and the only social context in which she can function. But it is not the real world.

What Lessing signals with one of the ramifications of the tree image is her desire to use Martha's particular history to make larger thematic statements about the relationship between the individual and society. But Martha can become an exemplary hero only if Lessing ignores her peculiar limitations. Lessing makes Martha exemplary by participating in her delusion that Mark's house represents society.

Although Martha's growth to mature identity has been the subject of all five volumes of *Children of Violence*, it is *The Four-Gated City* that Lessing has specifically labeled a *bildungsroman*. She prefaces that final volume of the series with a quotation from the ecologist Rachel Carson, which must be examined in detail if we are to understand her conception of the genre and her intention in *The Four-Gated City*:

> In its being and its meaning, this coast represents not merely an uneasy equilibrium of land and water masses; it is eloquent of a continuing change now actually in progress, a change being brought about by the life processes of living things. Perhaps the sense of this comes most clearly to one standing on a bridge between the Keys, looking out over miles of water, dotted with mangrove-covered islands to the horizon. . . . Under the bridge a green mangrove seedling floats, long and slender, one end already beginning to show the development of roots, beginning to reach down through the water, ready to grasp and to root firmly in any muddy shoal that may lie across its path. Over the years the mangroves bridge the water gaps between the islands; they extend the mainland; they create new islands. . . . So this coast is built.

The mangrove is a fresh and vivid image for the protagonist of a *bildungsroman*, whose development depends equally on the little something within and the outward pressure of events, whose aerial roots finally embed themselves in the mire of everyday. Furthermore, the mangrove is an Eriksonian image of the hero who reconciles the disharmony between his individuality and a society which is uncongenial to it by creating new social configurations, thus extending the mainland. Clearly, Lessing has the mangrove in mind in her depiction of Martha and her relationship to others. Like that tree, Martha has aerial roots; her consciousness needs the freedom of open space in which to develop. But her roots must be grounded in the muddy complexities of Mark's household if she is to grow to her full potential. And if, in the appendix to *The Four-Gated City*, Martha does not create a new island, she participates in the creation of a new and harmonious society on the island Lessing gives her.

Lessing is commonly spoken of as an intellectual novelist. I do not understand that to mean that she writes novels of ideas. What makes her an intellectual writer is not so much the content of her ideas or their primacy but her method of embodying them in her novels. Like Donne the preacher, Lessing conveys thematic statement through metaphor. As we have seen in examining *Children of Violence*, she uses metaphor both to clarify and adumbrate meaning. *Children of Violence* is, finally, a flawed *bildungsroman* because of a failure of intellect, because the two metaphors that control the meaning of *The Four-Gated City* and sum up the meaning of Martha's quest are at odds: the implications of one contradict the conclusions of the other.

The final ramification of the tree image, announced in the epigraph to the novel and embodied in the appendix, makes Martha a bridge to the future, the creator of new social configurations to replace the uncongenial forms of contemporary society. According to this extension of the tree metaphor, Martha, like Erikson's Luther, "although suffering and deviating dangerously through what appears to be a prolonged adolescence, eventually come[s] to contribute an original bit to an emerging style of life" (*Young Man Luther*, p. 15).

But in order to use the image of the mangrove tree to make this statement about Martha, Lessing has to ignore one aspect of the image. The mangrove tree creates new land because its roots are "ready to grasp and to root firmly in any muddy shoal that may lie across its path." Luther's original contribution was the consequence of the profound identification he could make between his individual neurosis and the revolutionary ferment of sixteenth-century Europe. Martha's inability to come to terms with the real world, which has been unmistakably asserted by Lessing's manipulation of the various aspects of the house metaphor, disqualifies her as a mangrove. Lessing can use that image to define Martha's final relationship with society only by willfully ignoring the implications of her metaphor.

Children of Violence is concerned with the theme of "the individual conscience in its relations with the collective." The individual whom Lessing has chosen to portray, Martha Quest, cannot realize the fullness of identity in relation to the collective that Lessing depicts as real. As the structure of related metaphors by which Lessing embodies the statement of the novels declares, this is in part because of that individual's idiosyncracies. But it is equally true that the collective, as Lessing describes it in *Children of Violence*, is hostile to the individual. The logical conclusion to the conflict between the two occurs at the end of Part Four of *The Four-Gated City*. It is a bleak and pessimistic acceptance of the irreconcilability of the self and society.

By sleight of hand, Lessing can end her investigation of Martha's quest for identity optimistically. By creating Utopia she can continue to make the Eriksonian assertion that the self and society are interdependent and mutually supportive. But in doing so she denies the ineluctability of the world we live in. In proposing a fictitious end to that world, in then creating on an island "off the northwest coast of Scotland" (FG, p. 596) an ideal society which duplicates Martha's temenos, Lessing has legitimized Martha's pathology. Her legerdemain betrays the humanism she shares with Erikson, who maintains that "psychosocial identity is necessary as the anchoring of man's transient existence in the here and the now" (*Identity*, p. 42). The perspective from which Lessing has surveyed Martha's growth is consistently Eriksonian in its insistence on the inescapable necessity for the individual to come to terms with reality in order to achieve a sense of identity. In sidestepping reality to conclude *The Four-Gated City*, Lessing commits an act of *mauvaise foi* upon herself as well as her readers.

7. AFTERWORD

It was not to test the hypothesis that Eriksonian ego-psychology may be the way out of a critical cul-de-sac reached by students of the *bildungs-roman* that I undertook an Eriksonian analysis of Doris Lessing's *Children of Violence*. Rather I was motivated by striking similarities between the way Martha Quest, Lessing's protagonist, describes the process of her growth and Erikson's description of psychosocial development. But the more deeply engrossed in Lessing's serial novel I became, the more convinced I grew that it must be seen as a uniquely contemporary representative of the genre to which Lessing has assigned it, the *bildungsroman*. Approaching the cruces of interpretation which have perplexed critics of *Children of Violence*—that its final volume, devoted to Martha's middle age, is the one Lessing specifically calls a *bildungsroman*, and that this final volume, hence the series, concludes with an apocalypse—I saw that they were crucial not so much to an interpretation of Lessing's intention and achievement in these novels as to an understanding of what form a contemporary *bildungsroman* can and will most likely take.

What the preceding chapters record is a journey toward one destination that turned out in the end to arrive there, but not only there. I now see that the terminus from which this brief excursion into psychological criticism departed was constructed by T. S. Eliot, who propounded the paradox that the critic "will not find it preposterous that the past should be altered by the present as much as the present is directed by the past."[1] The critical past that I seem to have altered is classical psychoanalytic criticism, and by means of a critical present that declares as its first postulate an indebtedness to that past.

All contemporary criticism, whether "psychological" or not, has been altered and enriched in its response to literature by the findings of depth psychology. It has illuminated the introspective regions of fiction and poetry, given the critic a vocabulary and a context by and in which to understand the inner reality of fictional personae. But in focusing on individual dynamics, psychoanalysis may have restricted its utility to private fictions—to lyric poetry for example, or to what Mark Spilka has called the "projective novel, in which surface life reflects the inner self."[2]

In his contribution to the Wellfleet Papers,[3] Robert Jay Lifton observes that "there is in classical psychoanalysis an implicit assumption that the larger historical universe is *nothing but* a manifestation of the projections or emanations of the individual psyche. Or if not that, history is seen as a kind of featureless background for those projections and emanations—something 'out there' which is 'given,' but which does not significantly influence what is 'in here'" (p. 23). This, Lifton contends, has made history and psychology antipathetic disciplines, "even if we limit our observations to depth psychology and to man-centered history" (p. 23).

The Wellfleet symposium was designed by Lifton, Erik Erikson, and Kenneth Keniston to heal this breach between psychology—specifically depth psychology—and history. The transcript of its proceedings has been instructive to me, a critic who is concerned with the literary similacrum of history, the realistic novel of the nineteenth and early twentieth centuries. For however indispensable it may be in uncovering the dynamics of the individual characters, psychoanalytic criticism has not, to my satisfaction, comprehended what—in contradistinction to Spilka's "projective novel"—I would call contextual fictions, novels of a self or selves in society. As Erikson has observed, psychoanalysis has not developed terms to conceptualize the environment" (*Identity*, p. 24).

Like the case history, the psychoanalytic study of a contextual fiction tends to discount the character's "residence, ethnic background, and occupation" in order to arrive at "the essence of the inner dynamics" (*Identity*, p. 44). Thus psychoanalytic criticism, ignoring the accidents of environment, discerns the character type, the essential inner dynamics of a Hamlet, who is timeless and placeless and miraculously resurrected in *Sons and Lovers*, ignoring what Erikson would insist is the "relevance" to inner dynamics of the character's milieu—a hypothetical Denmark, a real Elizabethan or twentieth-century England.

It is because his reformulation of basic Freudian psychoanalysis *has* developed "terms to conceptualize the environment" that I found Erikson's theory valuable in approaching the genre with which I had to contend in coming to terms with *Children of Violence*.

It might be argued that the *bildungsroman* is a species of the novel which psychoanalytic criticism is particularly fitted to examine. In his recent book on the English *bildungsroman*, Jerome Buckley prefaces his discussion of some dozen nineteenth- and twentieth-century novels by examining a poem. For, he says, "in tracing the 'growth of a poet's mind'" in *The Prelude*, Wordsworth "began with recollections of early childhood on the assumption, psychologically acute, that the child was father of the man."[4] This is the central assumption of classic psychoanalysis (an assumption

Erikson shares): the idiosyncratic contours of the adult are shaped in the crucible of early childhood. And since the childhoods of most *bildungshelden* are abundantly rendered in *bildungsromane*—one thinks of David Copperfield, Pip, Maggie Tulliver, Stephen Dedalus—the psychoanalytic critic is not only justified but virtually invited to study the growth of the protagonist in terms of infantile traumas.

To understand why, however brilliantly it may illuminate the growth of the protagonist, psychoanalytic criticism is not the ideal lamp for the student of *bildungsromane*, one need only return to the comments of Wilhelm Dilthey, who coined the name. In his 1906 essay on Hölderlin, Dilthey stressed the developmental aspect of bildung:

> [The *bildungsroman*] examines a regular course of development in the life of the individual; each of its stages has its own value and each is at the same time the basis of a higher stage. The dissonances and conflicts of life appear as the necessary transit points of the individual on his way to maturity and harmony.[5]

What strikes me about Dilthey's remarks on development is their Eriksonian resonance. The kind of development Dilthey discerned in the *bildungsroman* is precisely that normative development Erik Erikson describes in the "life cycle," his reformulation of Freudian psychosexual developmental theory. For Erikson, as for Dilthey, the individual grows to maturity by stages, each of which "has its own value and . . . is at the same time the basis of a higher stage" (*Identity*, p. 92). Dilthey's "dissonances and conflicts" are what Erikson calls "crises" in the individual's growth, epiphanic moments that do not provide final illumination but instead mark a "turning point"; the resolution of one crisis forms the basis of continued growth.

What the protagonist of a *bildungsroman* is developing, what he is growing toward, is a sense of what Dilthey calls "maturity and harmony." Roy Pascal, in his discussion of the first *bildungsroman*, defines this maturity as the "personal self-fulfilment" Wilhelm Meister achieves at that "moment when he ceases to be self-centred and becomes society-centred, thus beginning to shape his true self" (*The German Novel*, p. 11). The "true self" as opposed to what we might call the "given self" is what Wilhelm has in mind when he says, in the *Lehrjahre*, that his goal is "to develop myself entirely as I am." If he had always been all he was meant to be, there would be no need to develop. Wilhelm's task is to discover and realize his potential self, and to do this he must move from the mirror to the window, must forsake his childish puppet theater to enter the social drama.

Dilthey's "maturity" and Pascal's "self-fulfilment" are, for Erikson, "a sense of identity," which for him—as for Pascal—is "located in the core of the individual and yet also in the core of his communal culture." The process by which an individual arrives at a sense of his true self "establishes, in fact, the identity of those two identities" (*Identity*, p. 22). Erikson untangles this paradox by referring to two mature persons and their articulation of their sense of identity. For William James identity means a sense of what is "most deeply and intensely active and alive" in himself, a "voice inside which speaks and says: '*This* is the real me!'" (p. 19). This "real me," which Erikson describes as "a subjective sense of an invigorating sameness and continuity," is the "I am" which Wilhelm Meister seeks to develop. In the words of a latter day *bildungsheld*, it is "the little something within" which makes the individual unique.

But Hans Castorp knew that "the little something within" emerges into self-consciousness only by continually responding to the "outward pressure" of events. It is finally to be defined only in relation to some outer world, as Erikson's second spokesman for identity realized when he allied his sense of himself with his identity as a Jew. In a speech to the Vienna B'nai B'rith in 1926, Freud acknowledged the "common mental construction" which united him with all Jews in his "clear consciousness of inner identity." This "unity of personal and cultural identity," as Erikson terms it (p. 20), is in part what Pascal has in mind when he speaks of Wilhelm Meister's discovery of his "true self." For Wilhelm, as for Erikson's Freud, it is achieved by a movement from self to self-in-society.

Erikson gets from self to society by moving from zones to modes. Classic psychoanalysis charts human development as a movement of energy from one body zone to another—from mouth to anus to genitals. In his revision of Freud's theory of infantile sexuality,[6] however, Erikson saw that while a stage in human development might be said to have a "zonal aspect because it concerns a body zone," it may have the "quality" of that zone even when it is not specifically manifested physically. This quality Erikson called the "mode aspect" of development, or "modality." To illustrate, he discussed the case of a little girl who was brought to him because of her extreme resistance to toilet training. Erikson went beyond the analysis of the pleasure involved for the little girl in controlling her sphincters, beyond the aggression to her mother which her refusal to control her sphincters enabled her to express, to observe that "this child's behavior, even where it is not anal in a zonal sense, has the quality of a sphincter problem." What Erikson then describes as an anal modality is an "alternation of holding on and letting go, of withholding and giving, of opening up and closing up," in short "retentive and eliminative modes" of behavior.

Grounded as it is in Freud's theory of psychosexual development, even using Freudian terminology, Erikson's theory may not seem, at first glance, to differ significantly from its model. But the difference is there, in the shift from the personal to the public which occurs in the shift from zone to mode.

For a zone is a part of one's body, but a mode is a form of behavior, and, moreover, social behavior. One retains or eliminates, not merely because such actions are pleasurable but because they seem the appropriate responses to the world, conceived of as hostile or benevolent or, more likely, some volatile mixture of the two. While acknowledging that psychoanalysis must remain grounded in "its basic biological formulations," Erikson proceeds to chart development as a series of encounters between "the nervous excitability as well as the co-ordination of the 'erogenous' organs" and the "selective reactivity of significant people in the environment." What is, in classical psychoanalysis, "a vague surrounding 'outer world' of arbitrary and hostile social conventions" becomes, for Erikson, one of the indispensable factors in individual development.

"We cannot even begin to encompass the human life cycle," Erikson writes in *Young Man Luther*, "without learning to account for the fact that a human being under observation has grown stage by stage into a social world; this world, always for worse *and* for better, has step by step prepared for him an outer reality made up of human traditions and institutions which utilize and thus nourish his developing capacities, attract and modulate his drives, respond to and delimit his fears and phantasies, and assign to him a position in life appropriate to his psychosocial powers" (p. 20). His study of Luther demonstrates this thesis, indicating how far and in what directions Erikson's theory of development goes beyond Freud. More importantly for my purposes, the Luther book also suggests the utility to the literary critic of Erikson's formulation of the development toward identity or, as Dilthey would prefer to call it, maturity. *Young Man Luther* is a very particular kind of biography; it is a nonfictional *bildungsroman*.

Erikson is not the first, of course, to note Luther's characteristic anality. But his treatment of it moves beyond its zonal manifestation (his "lifelong constipation and urine retention," p. 205) to consider how anal modalities dominate Luther's behavior. "In supplementing Freud's scheme of infantile psychosexual stages," Erikson says, "I have suggested a psychosocial scheme in which the stage characterized by Freud's *anality* also serves to establish psychosocial *autonomy* which can and does mean independence, but does and can also mean defiance, stubbornness, self-insistence" (p. 122). Luther's anal modality, an alternation of "retention and elimination" (p. 205), is manifested most clearly during his adolescent crisis of identity, when "he changed from a highly restrained and retentive individual into an explosive person; [as a monk] he had found an unexpected release of self-expression and with it, of the many-sided power of his personality" (p. 205).

Erikson grounds Luther's idiosyncratic modality in his ambivalent relationship to his father. "No doubt when Martin learned to speak up, much that he had to say to the devil was fueled by a highly-compressed store of defiance consisting of what he had been unable to say to his father" (p. 122). The family nexus of neurosis is, of course, a central tenet of psychoanalysis. Where Erikson supplements Freud is in his recognition that Luther's relationship to his father was a microcosmic relationship, that it exemplified and reiterated the contemporary relationship of the individual to society. Luther's "peculiarly tenacious problem of the domestic relationship to his own father" reflected and was part of a larger ideological crisis that characterized sixteenth-century Germany in particular and pre-Reformation Europe in general, "a crisis about the theory and practice, the power and responsibility, of the moral authority invested in father; on earth and in heaven; at home, in the market-place, and in politics; in the castles, the capitals, and in Rome" (p. 77). Thus Luther's modality was, in a sense, typical of the sensitive individual's response to his society. In other words, Luther was an exemplary man, like the *bildungsheld,* whom Georg Lukács calls an "accidental" hero, "picked out of an unlimited number of men who share his aspirations, and . . . placed at the centre of the narrative . . . because his seeking and finding reveal the world's totality more clearly" (*The Theory of the Novel,* p. 134).

As they are worked out in *Young Man Luther,* Erikson's descriptive categories provide three vantage points from which individual development can be observed and described. First the individual's development is understood in its most fundamental and private character, which for Erikson is essentially Freudian, essentially psychosexual. This universal pattern of development is then particularized according to the specific local environment of the individual, his family. Again this second way of describing development, like the first, is essentially Freudian. It is the framework into which the Oedipal configuration fits; the particular family is a manifestation of a universal and repeated pattern, just as individual growth is a particular manifestation of a universal sequence of development. These two perspectives combine to form the vantage point of the psychoanalytic critic.

In moving beyond this point, Erikson creates new critical perspectives. To understand and describe the development of an individual—in this case Luther—he moves from the universally human to the accidental and historical, without losing sight of what can be viewed most distinctly from the vantage point of psychoanalysis. This simultaneous attention to what Erikson has called "individual life cycles, the sequence of generations, and the structure of society" (*Identity,* p. 141) is what makes Eriksonian psychology so eminently suited to the critical examination of *bildungsromane.* For these fictions are similarly concerned to document the growth of the protagonist as the particularization of a universal process, particularized by the uniqueness not only of the hero and his family, but of the world he inhabits. One student of the genre has called the primary experience of the *bildungsroman* "man and his meeting with the world, Mundus et Infans."[7] It is that meeting that Eriksonian psychology illuminates.

Using an Eriksonian lamp, we may be able to shed new light on questions about this problematic genre raised by nonpsychological critics. For instance, scholars have discerned a significant and, for many, perplexing distinction between *Wilhelm Meister* and later *bildungsromane.* In a recent article David H. Miles notes that the distinctive feature of the classic, eighteenth century *bildungsroman* is "the hero's ultimate assimilation into existing society."[8] Earlier Georg Lukács had said much the same thing when he noted that the hero of the classic *bildungsroman* found "responses to the innermost demands of his soul in the structures of society" (*Theory of the Novel*, p. 133). Yet in what Miles calls "the post-classical period" of the nineteenth and twentieth centuries, the protagonist is a hero insofar as he rebels against society. He discovers, according to Lukács, that "the desire for essence always leads out of the world of social structures." If Lothario's "hier oder nirgends ist Amerika" is the touchstone of the classic *bildungsroman,* Stephen Dedalus' "non serviam" is the typical cry of its romantic successor.

Testing always by the standard of the prototype, *Wilhelm Meister,* critics ask: Can a novel whose hero either scorns to enter or is denied admission by society properly be called a *bildungsroman?* In an increasingly chaotic and incomprehensible world, is *bildung* possible? Miles concludes, after surveying his candidates for contemporary *bildungsromane,* that he can see "some sort of absolute end to the genre." Certainly at this point *discussion* of the genre has reached a dead end.

But if we define *bildung* as a quest for what Erikson calls identity, the shift from classic to romantic *bildungsroman* becomes explicable. According to him, the individual achieves a sense of identity when he becomes aware that "there is a self-sameness and continuity . . . to the style of [his] individuality and that this style coincides with the sameness and continuity of [his] meaning for significant others in the immediate community" (*Identity*, p. 50). Or in Lukács' words, he finds "responses to the innermost demands of his soul in the structures of society." The individual's sense of himself, confirmed by his society, is the identity with which he enters that society and takes his place as an adult, "beyond identity" in Erikson's life cycle. Clearly this is the pattern of *Wilhelm Meister,* a pattern that becomes distorted and finally unusable as the nineteenth century moves into the twentieth, as society becomes both anonymous and heterogeneous, distinctly hostile to the individual, who feels alienated, "hurled back upon himself," in Theodore Ziolkowski's words, "as the sole authority."[9]

What Erikson's studies of adolescents, both historical and contemporary, reveal is that "the identity problem . . . changes with the historical period" (p. 27). Thus, while the basic formulation of the sense of identity—that it consists in the social corroboration of one's sense of individuality—is directly applicable to the prototypical *bildungsroman, Wilhelm Meister,* it may not be limited to that application. Identity may not be a stable commodity, produced when, and only when, the ingredients of self-awareness and social confirmation are mixed in the prescribed proportions. With this in mind, the critic can turn afresh to postclassical *bildungsromane.* Instead of wondering, "can a hero achieve a sense of identity in a hostile world," he can more fruitfully ask, "what sort of identity can the hero achieve in an uncongenial society."

This, at any rate, is the sort of question I found myself asking of *Children of Violence.* I do not think that Lessing has answered it satisfactorily, but it is the question she raises. *Children of Violence* is a problematic *bildungsroman,* but by Eriksonian standards it is a genuine one. The old stable order of Wilhelm Meister's world is shattered; it is no longer available to confirm and contain the creative individual. As a contemporary *bildungsroman, The Four-Gated City* goes beyond the despair of nineteenth-century *bildungsromane* to explore the Eriksonian suggestion that the inhospitable world we live in may, however, be seen "not as an imposed hostile reality, but as a potential promise for a more universal human identity" (p. 66).

WORKS CITED

Bachelard, Gaston, *The Poetics of Space* (1958), trans. Maria Jolas (1964), Boston, Beacon Press, 1969.

Blake, Peter, *The Master Builders*, New York, Alfred A. Knopf, 1961.

Buckley, Jerome Hamilton, *Season of Youth: The Bildungsroman from Dickens to Golding*, Cambridge, Mass., Harvard University Press, 1974.

Eliot, T. S., "Tradition and the Individual Talent," *Selected Essays*, 3rd enlarged ed., London, Faber and Faber, 1951.

Erikson, Erik H., *Childhood and Society*, 2nd ed., New York, W. W. Norton, 1963.

——, *Gandhi's Truth: On the Origins of Militant Nonviolence*, New York, W. W. Norton, 1969.

——, *Identity: Youth and Crisis*, New York, W. W. Norton, 1968.

——, *Insight and Responsibility*, New York, W. W. Norton, 1964.

——, *Young Man Luther: A Study in Psychoanalysis and History* (1958), New York, Norton Library, 1962.

Evans, Richard I., *Dialogue with Erik Erikson*, New York, E. P. Dutton, 1969.

Goethe, Johann Wolfgang von, *Wilhelm Meister's Apprenticeship* (1795-96), trans. Thomas Carlyle (1824), New York, Collier Books, 1962.

Hardin, Nancy Shields, "Doris Lessing and the Sufi Way," *Contemporary Literature*, 14, No. 4 (Autumn 1973), 565-581.

Howe, Susanne, *Wilhelm Meister and His English Kinsmen*, New York, Columbia University Press, 1930.

Kaplan, Sydney Janet, "The Limits of Consciousness in the Novels of Doris Lessing," *Contemporary Literature*, 14, No. 4 (Autumn 1973), 536-549.

Karl, Frederick R., "Doris Lessing in the Sixties: The New Anatomy of Melancholy," *Contemporary Literature*, 13, No. 1 (Winter 1972), 15-33.

Laing, R. D., *The Divided Self: An Existential Study in Sanity and Madness* (1959), London, Pelican Books, 1965.

——, *The Politics of Experience*, New York, Ballantine Books, 1967.

Lessing, Doris, *Briefing for a Descent into Hell*, New York, Alfred A. Knopf, 1971.

——, *Martha Quest* (1952), New York, New American Library, 1970.

——, *A Proper Marriage* (1954), New York, New American Library, 1970.

——, *A Ripple From the Storm* (1958), New York, New American Library, 1970.

——, *Landlocked* (1965), New York, New American Library, 1970.

——, *The Four-Gated City* (1969), New York, Alfred A. Knopf, 1969.

——, *The Golden Notebook*, New York, Simon and Schuster, 1962.

——, "On the Golden Notebook," *Partisan Review*, 40, No. 1 (Winter 1973), 14-30.

——, "The Small Personal Voice," *Declaration*, ed. Tom Maschler, London, MacGibbon and Kee, 1957.

——, *A Small Personal Voice*, New York, Alfred A. Knopf, 1974.

——, *The Summer before The Dark*, New York, Alfred A. Knopf, 1973.

Lifton, Robert Jay, with Eric Olson, eds., *Explorations in Psychohistory: The Wellfleet Papers*, New York, Simon and Schuster, 1974.

Lukács, Georg, *The Theory of the Novel: A Historico-Philosophical Essay on the Forms of Great Epic Literature* (1920), trans. Anna Bostock, Cambridge, Mass., M.I.T. Press, 1971.

Mann, Thomas, *The Magic Mountain* (1924), trans. H. T. Lowe-Porter (1927), New York, Vintage Books, 1969.

Miles, David H., "The Picaro's Journey to the Confessional: The Changing Image of the Hero in the German Bildungsroman," *PMLA*, 89, No. 5 (October 1974), 980–992.

Newquist, Roy, *Counterpoint*, New York, Simon and Schuster, 1964.

Pascal, Roy, *The German Novel: Studies*, Toronto, University of Toronto Press, 1956.

Ricoeur, Paul, "Hermeneutics: The Approaches to Symbol," trans. Denis Savage, *European Literary Theory and Practice: From Existential Phenomenology to Structuralism*, ed. Vernon W. Gras (New York, Delta Book, 1973), pp. 87–117.

Sadler, William A., Jr., *Existence and Love*, New York, Scribners, 1969.

Schlueter, Paul, *The Novels of Doris Lessing*, Carbondale, Ill., Southern Illinois University Press, 1973.

Spacks, Patricia Meyer, "Free Women," *Hudson Review*, 24 (Winter 1971–72), 559–573.

Spilka, Mark, "David Copperfield as Psychological Fiction," *Critical Quarterly*, 1, No. 4 (Winter 1959), 292–301.

Tennyson, G. B., "The Bildungsroman in Nineteenth-Century English Literature," in *Medieval Epic to the "Epic Theater" of Brecht*, ed. Rosario P. Armato and John M. Spalek (Los Angeles, University of Southern California Press, 1968), pp. 135–146.

Van Ghent, Dorothy, *The English Novel: Form and Function*, New York, Holt, Rinehart and Winston, 1953.

Ziolkowski, Theodore, *The Novels of Hermann Hesse: A Study in Theme and Structure*, Princeton, N.J., Princeton University Press, 1967.

NOTES

1. ERIKSON AND THE BILDUNGSROMAN

1. Doris Lessing, *The Four-Gated City* (New York: Alfred A. Knopf, 1969), p. 615. Further references to this novel (abbreviated FG) will be incorporated in the text.

2. Johann Wolfgang von Goethe, *Wilhelm Meister's Apprenticeship* (1795-96), trans. Thomas Carlyle (1824; rpt. New York: Collier Books, 1962), p. 274. Further references will be to this edition and will be incorporated in the text.

3. Paul Schlueter, *The Novels of Doris Lessing* (Carbondale, Ill.: Southern Illinois University Press, 1973), p. 75.

4. Erik H. Erikson, *Identity: Youth and Crisis* (New York: W. W. Norton & Company, Inc., 1968), p. 83. Further references will be abbreviated as *Identity* and incorporated in the text.

5. Thomas Mann, *The Magic Mountain* (1924), trans. H. T. Lowe-Porter (1927; rpt. New York: Vintage Books, 1969), p. 596.

6. Doris Lessing, *A Proper Marriage* (1954; rpt. New York: New American Library, 1970), pp. 274-275. Further references will be to this edition (abbreviated PM) and will be incorporated in the text.

7. Doris Lessing, *A Ripple From the Storm* (1958; rpt. New York: New American Library, 1970), p. 19. Further reference will be to this edition (abbreviated RS) and will be incorporated in the text.

8. Georg Lukács, *The Theory of the Novel: A Historico-philosophical Essay on the Forms of Great Epic Literature* (1920), trans. Anna Bostock (Cambridge, Mass.: The M.I.T. Press, 1971), p. 133. Further references will be to Lukács and will be incorporated in the text.

9. Shakespeare always excepted. It is Jarno, a member of the Society of the Tower, who introduces Wilhelm to his works, which Wilhelm declares "incite me, more than anything beside, to quicken my footsteps forwards into the actual world." (p. 188)

10. Erik H. Erikson, *Young Man Luther: A Study in Psychoanalysis and History* (1958; rpt. New York: The Norton Library, 1962), p. 67. Further references will be incorporated in the text.

11. Erik H. Erikson, *Childhood and Society*, 2nd ed. (New York: W. W. Norton & Company, Inc., 1963), p. 45. Further references will be to this edition and will be incorporated in the text.

2. THE EPIGENESIS OF MARTHA'S IDENTITY

1. R. D. Laing, *The Divided Self: An Existential Study in Sanity and Madness* (1959; rpt. London: Pelican Books, 1965), p. 17. Subsequent references will be to this edition and will be incorporated in the text.

2. Even the heroes of post-Goethian novels of education, living in an uncongenial society, think it essential to assert their identities and to be recognized, even if they are then rejected, by their fellows. Sometimes, as preeminently with Stephen Dedalus, their need to make an impression on their world leads them to bizarre and flamboyant excesses of gesture and behavior.

3. And for Laing, as well as for Erikson, the schizoid personality is characterized by orality. See *The Divided Self*, p. 145.

4. Martha thinks of food almost anthropomorphically. She endows it with the power to make her fat, despite her conscious efforts to be slim. It is her enemy, and as this passage from *Martha Quest* indicates, she believes it is stronger than she. Characteristically passive, Martha is bewildered by her consistent gain in weight, failing to assume responsibility for her own caloric intake:

> This business of food: how little one should take it for granted! . . . she could not eat without feeling guilty and promising restitution to herself by giving up the next meal. On the other

hand, she would suddenly turn aside into a shop, without even knowing she had intended to, and buy half a dozen slabs of chocolate, which she would eat, secretly, until she was sickened and very alarmed, saying she must be careful, for she would certainly lose her figure if she went on like this.

Martha Quest (1952; rpt. New York: New American Library, 1970), p. 110. Further references will be to this edition (abbreviated MQ) and will be incorporated in the text.

After Caroline's birth, Martha fights her enemy and wins: "And now Martha was free again, she proceeded to starve herself. By dint of literally not eating anything, she had lost twenty pounds at the end of six weeks." (PM, p. 158) The notes of hostility and triumph in this brief passage are incomprehensible unless we understand the degree to which Martha has reified food.

5. This is almost graphically illustrated in the opening chapter of *Landlocked*, when the hungry Martha refuses dinner first with Joss and Solly Cohen, then with Thomas Stern, and finally with her mother until, at the end of the evening, she returns home to Anton, with whom she would "drink for an hour or so, have dinner, listen to the band, and in this way both could forget (Martha hoped) the implications of the fact that practically everything he said, or did, these days, was really a reproach for her not doing, or being, what he now wanted her to be." *Landlocked* (1965: rpt. New York: New American Library, 1970), p. 40. Subsequent references will be to this edition (abbreviated LL) and will be incorporated in the text. See also FG, pp. 14, 77, and 259 for further instances of Martha's communication by eating, here the fried bread and strong tea she shares with the dockers and with Iris and Jimmy, or the "small bits of cake" she and her mother nibble "to please the other."

6. Martha asserts her "freedom" from the biological confinements of pregnancy and maternity by weaning Caroline and going on a rigorous diet (PM, p. 158). Then she begins a campaign to free herself from Caroline. As long as it bothers her that the child doesn't eat, she feels tied to her, and "she must break this bond!" (PM, p. 202) By subduing her natural impulses, Martha succeeds: "Now she was able to cook the food and serve Caroline with it and not care if she ate it or not." (PM, pp. 204–205) She acknowledges even to herself that more than nutrition has been at issue: "She became perversely sad because she had won the victory. It seemed that something must have snapped between her and her daughter." (PM, p. 205) What she does not realize is that her behavior was dictated by her unconscious needs rather than by a rational sense of what was best for Caroline.

7. Erik H. Erikson, *Insight and Responsibility* (New York: W. W. Norton & Company, Inc., 1964), p. 117. Further references will be incorporated in the text.

8. Roy Newquist, *Counterpoint* (New York: Simon and Schuster, 1964), p. 423. This interview has been reprinted in Doris Lessing, *A Small Personal Voice* (New York: Alfred A. Knopf, 1974), pp. 45–60.

9. William A. Sadler, Jr., *Existence and Love* (New York: Scribner, 1969), p. 107.

10. She undergoes repeated bouts of self-willed "starvation" to mold her body into a shape others define as attractive.

11. "Shame supposes that one is completely exposed and conscious of being looked at . . . in dreams of shame we are stared at in a condition of incomplete dress." (*Identity*, p. 110)

12. Roy Pascal, *The German Novel: Studies* (Toronto: University of Toronto Press, 1956), p. 23. Subsequent references will be incorporated in the text.

13. Lessing's ironic portrayal of a Martha who says one thing and does another should caution critics against accepting Martha as Lessing's spokesman. What is only a venial critical sin in the early volumes of *Children of Violence*, when presumably Martha's generally liberal sentiments more or less reflect her creator's, becomes an insuperable bar to assessing *Landlocked* and *The Four-Gated City*. Only by distinguishing scrupulously between Martha and Lessing is it possible to determine to what degree the author shares her protagonist's definition and attitude toward reality. It will become apparent that this is the crucial question in any final evaluation of *Children of Violence*.

3. MARTHA AND THE UNCONGENIAL SOCIETY

1. Mrs. Quest's dream of giving birth to herself resembles the birth imagery of Martha's illumination, and recalls Lessing's mescaline dream in which she "invented" a birth for herself that cancelled the effect of her own actual birth, which was "painful and bad." This raises the inescapable question of the pathological dimensions of artistic creation. In *Children of Violence,* Lessing seems to condemn the delusional and unrealistic creativity of both Martha and her mother. May Quest's fictions, by obscuring and even denying reality, hinder Martha in her quest for the truth about herself and the world she lives in. Martha's own attempts to create an image of her self are marked by a similar

tendency to fabricate, rather than render, reality. But is not Lessing, who associates her dream of giving birth to herself with "the process of creative writing," equally open to the criticism she makes of her characters when she ends *Children of Violence* by giving form to her fantasy? The line between giving form and giving the lie is the subject of Anna Wulf's agonized introspections in *The Golden Notebook*, and as recently as 1973, Lessing expressed her dissatisfaction with her novels in terms Anna would understand: "How little I have managed to say of the truth, how little I have caught of all that complexity; how can this small neat thing be true when what I experienced was so rough and apparently formless and unshaped." Doris Lessing, "On the Golden Notebook," *Partisan Review*, 40, No.1 (Winter, 1973), 21.

2. In his "psycho-history" of Mohandas Gandhi, which is a kind of nonfictional *bildungsroman* in its attempt to account for the origins of Gandhi's charismatic leadership, Erikson observes that certain "leading individuals" exhibit "a premature conscience development and an early assumption of moral responsibility for a parent—a responsibility which they subsequently [extend] to mankind itself." Erik H. Erikson, *Gandhi's Truth: On the Origins of Militant Nonviolence* (New York: W. W. Norton & Company, Inc., 1969), p. 123. Subsequent references will be incorporated in the text.

In *Children of Violence*, both Martha and Francis exhibit this characteristic of the leader or, in fictional terms, hero. Martha, no less than Francis, makes allowances for her inadequate parent. In *Landlocked*, she observes that "the essence of [her] relationship with her mother must be, must, apparently, for ever be, that Mrs. Quest 'couldn't help it.' Well, she couldn't." (p. 12) And it is Martha and her therapist, Dr. Lamb, who finally bring Mrs. Quest to terms with her neuroses. (FG, pp. 272–273) Both Martha and Francis, in the appendix to *The Four-Gated City*, extend this sense of responsibility beyond their nuclear families to the children of the future, thus becoming "leaders" analogous to Gandhi. For Lessing, as well as for Erikson, the apex of the life cycle is not adolescent identity, but mature generativity.

4. MARTHA AND HER METAPHORS

1. Gandhi, like Martha, spent his youth on the "engrossing experiments" of "what to take in . . . in order to keep the inner man uncorrupted, and what to wear in order to present to the world the outer man that might represent the inner man." (*Gandhi's Truth*, p. 143) Food and dress are for the heroes of both these *bildungsromane* more than nourishment and covering; they are emblems of identity.

2. Later, more confident of herself, Martha discovers that "she had gone way out past any buoys, lighthouses, or charted points in her knowledge of herself." (FG, p. 62)

3. R. D. Laing, *The Politics of Experience* (New York: Ballantine Books, 1967), p. 120. Subsequent references will be incorporated in the text.

4. As Sydney Kaplan has observed in a more general discussion of Lessing's conception of individual consciousness, "the landscape of the mind itself resembles more the vastness and dryness of Africa than the water-soaked, protected isles of Great Britain. The usual metaphors for consciousness, streams and fountains" are replaced "by those of plains and vast spaces." Sydney Janet Kaplan, "The Limits of Consciousness in the Novels of Doris Lessing," *Contemporary Literature*, 14, No. 4 (Autumn 1973), 538.

5. MARTHA IN SOCIETY

1. Gaston Bachelard, *The Poetics of Space* (1958), trans. Maria Jolas (1964; rpt. Boston: Beacon Press, 1969), p. 91. Further references will be incorporated in the text.

2. This is a verbal echo of Martha's image of herself as "a shell of substance."

3. Paul Ricoeur, "Hermeneutics: The Approaches to Symbol," trans Denis Savage, in *European Literary Theory and Practice: From Existential Phenomenology to Structuralism*, ed. Vernon W. Gras (New York: Delta Book, 1973), pp. 87–117. Further references will be incorporated in the text.

4. Peter Blake, *The Master Builders* (New York: Alfred A. Knopf, 1961), p. 308. Further references will be incorporated in the text.

5. The positive aspects of being stripped and flayed (another word Lessing uses to describe Mark's disenchantment with Ottery Bartlett and the old order) are even more comprehensively examined in *The Summer before the Dark*.

6. THE END OF THE QUEST

1. Patricia Meyer Spacks, "Free Women," *Hudson Review*, 24 (Winter 1971–72), 570.

2. In 1957, Lessing stated that this relationship was the theme of *Children of Violence.* See Doris Lessing, "The Small Personal Voice," in *Declaration*, ed. Tom Maschler (London: MacGibbon and Kee, 1957), p. 22. This essay has been reprinted in Doris Lessing, *A Small Personal Voice* (New York: Alfred A. Knopf, 1974), pp. 3–21.

3. Spacks thinks, on the contrary, that *The Four-Gated City* claims that "solipsism, multiplied, may save the world." ("Free Women," 571)

4. As Nancy Hardin points out in a recent article, Sufism teaches that the way to enlightenment and self-realization is a dialectic between meditation and participation in the world:

> The Sufi is characterized by the slogan: "Be *in* the world but not *of* it." Participation in the world is primary, for the Sufi is one who excels in a trade or skill; although, the individual student is offered a "secret garden," wherein he may perfect his understanding and experience: "It is the development of the human being which counts, nothing else." Enlightenment comes only through experience, not by way of intellect: "He who tastes not, knows not."

Nancy Shields Hardin, "Doris Lessing and the Sufi Way," *Contemporary Literature* 14, No. 4 (Autumn 1973), 567. The compatibility of this doctrine with Eriksonian psychology should be self-evident. Lessing's attraction to Sufism, like her interest in Laingian psychiatry, in no way contradicts her essential humanism, which allies her fundamentally with Erikson.

5. Richard I. Evans, *Dialogue with Erik Erikson* (New York: E. P. Dutton & Co., Inc., 1969), p. 50.

6. It has, most convincingly, been argued by Spacks in "Free Women" and by Frederick R. Karl in "Doris Lessing in the Sixties: The New Anatomy of Melancholy," *Contemporary Literature*, 13, No. 1 (Winter 1972), 15–33. Karl's article is especially provocative in its analysis of *The Golden Notebook* and *The Four-Gated City* as examples of "literature of enclosure."

7. Dorothy Van Ghent, *The English Novel: Form and Function* (New York: Holt, Rinehart and Winston, 1953), p. 228.

7. AFTERWORD

1. "Tradition and the Individual Talent," *Selected Essays*, 3rd enlarged ed. (London: Faber and Faber, 1951), p. 15.

2. "David Copperfield as Psychological Fiction," *Critical Quarterly*, I, no. 4 (Winter 1959), 292.

3. *Explorations in Psychohistory: The Wellfleet Papers*, ed. Robert Jay Lifton with Eric Olson (New York: Simon and Schuster, 1974). See Lifton's paper, "On Psychohistory," pp. 21–41.

4. Jerome Hamilton Buckley, *Season of Youth: The Bildungsroman from Dickens to Golding* (Cambridge, Mass.: Harvard University Press, 1974), p. 4.

5. Quoted in G. B. Tennyson, "The Bildungsroman in Nineteenth-century English Literature," in *Medieval Epic to the "Epic Theater" of Brecht*, ed. Rosario P. Armato and John M. Spalek (Los Angeles: University of Southern California Press, 1968), p. 136.

6. I am here referring specifically to pp. 48–108 of *Childhood and Society*.

7. Susanne Howe, *Wilhelm Meister and His English Kinsmen* (New York, Columbia University Press, 1930), p. 1.

8. David H. Miles, "The Picaro's Journey to the Confessional: The Changing Image of the Hero in the German Bildungsroman," *PMLA*, 89, No. 5 (October 1974), 980–992.

9. *The Novels of Hermann Hesse: A Study in Theme and Structure* (Princeton, N.J.: Princeton University Press, 1967), p. 357.

INDEX